ONE STEP CLOSER

From Xero to #1: Becoming Linkin Park

JEFF BLUE

PERMUTED
PRESS

A PERMUTED PRESS BOOK
ISBN: 978-1-68261-967-4
ISBN (eBook): 978-1-68261-968-1

One Step Closer:
From Xero to #1: Becoming Linkin Park
© 2020 by Jeff Blue
All Rights Reserved

Cover art by Cody Corcoran
Interior design and layout by Sarah Heneghan, sarah-heneghan.com

Unless otherwise noted, all photos are courtesy of the author.

This is a work of nonfiction. All people, locations, events, and situations are portrayed to the best of the author's memory.

PERMUTED
PRESS

Permuted Press, LLC
New York • Nashville
permutedpress.com

Published in the United States of America
1 2 3 4 5 6 7 8 9 10

This book is dedicated to those who relentlessly pursue their dreams and make them a reality, and the few true friends we have in life who push us to be our best.

Thanks, Mom, Dad (RIP), Lee Lubin, David Rehman, Mojo and Dr. Chubbs (RIP), and Cannon.

CONTENTS

MEMBERS OF THE BAND
IN ALPHABETICAL ORDER

Chester Bennington

Rob Bourdon

Kyle Christener

Brad Delson

Dave Farrell

Joe Hahn

Scott Koziol

Mike Shinoda

Mark Wakefield

Surprising the band with their first gold record. Memorial Auditorium, Sacramento, CA. December 22, 2000.

FOREWORD

EAR READER,

I'm so proud to introduce you to my dear friend, Jeff Blue. Most folks don't know how many lives he has changed over the last few decades. I was there the moment Jeff reached out to Chester and changed our lives forever. If not for Jeff having been there from day one and having literally staked his career on them with Warner Bros., Xero's music would not have touched the lives of so many. We all know them now as Linkin Park and, after you read this book, you'll know them a lot better.

Thank you, Jeff, for having faith, the pure talent to recognize talent, and the passion and determination to make all of our dreams come true, especially when no one else believed. For all the fans, I know you will find Jeff's book inspirational and revelatory. You will get an inside look from someone who put all the ingredients together to launch Hybrid Theory into your hearts and minds. Jeff gave Chester the opportunity to share his angelic voice and Linkin Park the chance to share their singular musical vision with the world. My ex-husband and Linkin have been able to help multiple generations with their personal struggles as a result.

ONE STEP CLOSER

I will never forget where we came from or the individuals that helped make Linkin Park the household name it is today. My son, Draven, and I will always be grateful to Jeff for sharing these stories and giving people the opportunity to see Chester more as a person and not just a Rock Star. I'm truly honored to have experienced this journey with you!

With humble gratitude,
Samantha Bennington

ONE STEP CLOSER

CHAPTER 1

MY NEW INTERN

HEAD POUNDING AND EXHAUSTED, I STUMBLED INTO THE Zomba/Jive Music lobby. I was hit in the face by Nick Carter singing "As Long as You Love Me."

"It should be illegal to play Backstreet Boys before ten in the morning."

"It's almost ten-fifteen," a voice replied as I walked past the black carpet and red pleather sofas to the front desk. "Jeez, what happened to you?" our receptionist, Stephanie, asked as she handed me a stack of CDs with my name on them.

"The Interscope party is what happened," I tried to laugh.

"I thought you were lecturing at UCLA last night."

"I managed to achieve both objectives," I replied.

"Any luck finding an intern?" Stephanie asked.

"Everyone just wants school credit. I want someone with ambition and a good ear for music. Otherwise it's not worth the time," I said, walking away as the Backstreet Boys track continued blasting out of a colleague's office.

1

"By the way, there's a kid..." she shouted after me, but her voice was soon drowned out by the music.

Staggering past the rows of gold and platinum plaques adorning the walls, I turned the corner into my office when I was smacked in the leg by a Converse sneaker. Someone with a monster head of curly hair and dressed in camouflage shorts was spinning in my office chair. The stack of CDs flew out of my hands.

"What the hell? Who are you?" I asked, dumbfounded.

The mop of hair jumped up. Extending his hand, he said, "Oh my God, I'm so sorry. I'm Brad Delson. I was at your lecture last night."

As I limped toward my guest chair, my office phone rang. It was Stephanie. "Hey, I wasn't sure you heard me. There's someone waiting for you in your office. Said you were expecting him."

"No, I wasn't. At least, I don't think I was."

"I want an office like this someday. You've got a kick-ass drum set, guitars, keyboards, and a killer view of Sunset Boulevard. Pretty sick," Brad said enthusiastically.

"Whoa, back up. What are you doing in my office?"

"You said you were looking for an intern last night. Someone to help you develop your new artist, Macy Gray."

"Oh yeah. You were the only one who liked her demo. I remember the hair now," I chuckled. "You're lucky. I wasn't even going to come in until much later today. You would've missed me." I contemplated his mop of brown curly hair. Through my thudding headache, I remembered he actually had made some intelligent comments about Macy's music.

"Hey, you're still sitting in my chair. Get up," I said jokingly.

We began picking up the CDs, and he said, "I was really inspired by your lecture, Mister Blue."

"You can call me Jeff. Mr. Blue is my dad," I said jokingly.

He proceeded to tell me about growing up in Agoura, California, his upbringing, and his love for Metallica. His parents were pushing him into law school, but he wanted a career in music.

"Man, I've been there," I laughed. "Here's some free advice. Whatever you do, don't go to law school unless you're absolutely dying to be miserable."

He looked me up and down in my blue jeans and white T-shirt. "You get to dress like that every day?"

"Well, it is the music business. I save a ton on dry cleaning compared to lawyers," I said, as he glanced at my walls.

"That's a perk. So, what do you look for when you're signing an artist?" he asked.

"That's the million-dollar question," I said. "I look for identity, authenticity, an iconic voice, hit songs, and, of course, talent. But the difference between the most talented people and superstars is that the superstars are hungrier. They work harder and can deal with rejection. They'll do whatever it takes. That's who I want to work with."

"Well, I definitely have the drive." He studied the Korn plaque on my wall, and then pointed to a poster of Limp Bizkit. He rolled his eyes. "I'm going to create a band that blows them away. You'll see."

"Slow your roll. You're not even my intern yet and you're already dissing my bands? Plus, I've never heard of an internship turning into a record deal," I laughed.

Just then, Stephanie buzzed. "You got some messages this morning from UCLA students about the internship. You want to set up interviews?" I glanced at the phone and then back at Brad, who was holding my electric guitar. I saw a lot of myself in this kid.

At the same time, across town in Pasadena, a talented artist named Mike Shinoda was scribbling rap lyrics in his notebook, dreaming of taking his art to a new level. Four hundred miles away in Phoenix, Arizona, a skinny kid named Chester Bennington was getting inked with an exploding atom bomb tattoo on his back.

Not knowing what the universe was aligning at that moment, I replied, "Tell them it's filled, please."

Brad looked up from picking out a melody on the guitar and smiled. It was clear to me that he could play and that there was something special about him. It wasn't just his drive, intelligence, and extreme confidence. Something in my mind said, "This kid is a star." At that moment, we both knew my new intern was already in front of me; however, no one could have predicted where it would lead.

CHAPTER 2

FOLLOW YOUR GUT

It WAS EARLY NOVEMBER 1997. I HAD JUST CONVINCED ZOMBA Music Publishing to take a chance on Macy Gray even though she'd been dropped by her manager, her publisher, and her record label. I was certain she had the talent to be a star, but the music industry can be unforgiving. Once you're dropped, there's a stigma attached that's nearly impossible to overcome.

I had my head in my hands when Brad came in.

"What's wrong?" Brad asked.

"I'm just having a hard time getting A&R people to give Macy a chance."

"I'm trying to understand exactly what you do," he said. "It seems publishing is a lot like A&R, but it really isn't."

"That's an accurate yet ambiguous statement, Brad. Maybe you should go to law school after all," I laughed. "Here's your pop internship quiz. Tell me the difference between my job as a manager of creative at a publishing company compared to an A&R exec at a record label."

Brad pursed his lips. "Don't give me shit if I get this wrong, but the way I see it, your job as a publisher is to sign bands or artists; acquire a percentage of their copyright, or ownership, in the songs; register the songs with performance rights organizations such as BMI or ASCAP; collect royalties for performance and mechanicals, which are sales of the physical album; get placements for the songs in film and TV for fees, which is called synchronization, or synch licenses; and sometimes do development deals for artists who don't have any income stream from their songs yet."

"Ha, that's really good! I see you've been studying my UCLA lecture syllabus or you're reading off a cheat sheet right now. To clarify, the publisher's job is not to sign just the bands, but to sign the songwriters of the songs that the artist or band records and releases. In actuality, the songwriter may be the artist themselves or other contributing songwriters, beat makers, lyricists, anyone who has credit as a writer on a song. In regards to money, in a co-publishing deal, the publisher will give an advance to the writer to acquire half of the publishing the writer owns."

I grabbed a piece of paper and a pen and drew a large circle with a vertical line down the middle. "Think of the song as a pie. Split down the middle you've got two sets of rights: the publisher's share on one side and the writer's share on the other. You, as a songwriter, own both your writer's and publisher's share, but you can do a co-publishing deal where you transfer your rights to half of your publisher's share, which comes out to twenty-five percent of the entire pie, to a music publisher, like me, for a money advance, and we will collect and exploit your catalog."

"Right," he said rubbing his chin. "Okay, then what does the A&R executive at a record label do?"

"The A&R person discovers and signs the artist to the record label. They map out the plan with the label for the artist, choose the producer, decide which songs will be on the album, help with marketing, and function as the cheerleader slash liaison with all the other departments like radio, touring, publicity, et cetera."

"So, what you're doing with development is basically doing a publishing and A&R job in one, but you're only getting credit as the publisher?"

"My goal is to do A&R for a record label. If you have a dream, you gotta do whatever it takes to make it a reality. I'm paying my dues. I may fail along the way, but that's part of the life learning experience." Standing up, I said, "I hope you actually get something out of this internship. You're a really smart guy. Right now, I need to listen to the next demo. Maybe we can find a new band to sign to Zomba in that stack of demos. Let's work!"

CHAPTER 3

THE XERO CASSETTE

"CATCH!" HE SAID A LITTLE TOO LATE, AS A CASSETTE TAPE flew through the air, skidded across my desk, and knocked over a half-full can of Dr. Pepper.

"Way to make an entrance, Brad."

"Oops, sorry, man! You should hear this new music." He grabbed the cassette, popped it in the deck, and cranked the volume. Sitting back in my chair, I listened as Brad began wiping up the spill. "I'll just use this promo tee."

"That's the new Limp Bizkit T-shirt signed by the band for my birthday," I said, shaking my head.

I picked up the cassette case. "Xero?" I glanced at the artwork, which was a Xerox copy of what appeared to be a mountain. On the inside was a faded photo of four band members and a close-up photo of some guy. "No song titles? And who's this dude?"

"That's Mike, the rapper. Don't talk over the music," Brad replied half-jokingly. He rewound the tape. "Listen again from the start. This first song is called 'Fuse.'"

8

"Isn't that the intro from Disney's *Haunted House* album? I wore that record out in kindergarten!" I wasn't digging the song much at all.

The second song, with no title, incorporated a lot of hip hop. I loved the beat, the rapping was old school, and it had a simplistic guitar line with tasty harmonics that was instantly memorable. The song transitioned into an Alice in Chains–style chorus followed by a Rage Against the Machine–style guitar breakdown, with a hard-edged bridge that really impressed me.

"Is this one singer or two?"

"Rapper and a singer," Brad replied.

I flipped the tape over and played the third song, "Stick 'n' Move." My interest waned. The fourth song, "Reading My Eyes," however, pulled me back in. The rapper was talented, and I noticed an undeniable chemistry between him and the guitarist. There was something about the time signature that caught my attention as well, and I suddenly suspected it was Brad. I hoped it was Brad.

After the tape ended, Brad turned around. "Well?" he asked.

"It's cool," I said as I hit the eject button.

"That's it? What don't you like about it?"

"I didn't say I didn't like it. It has potential, but that guitarist sucks ass."

"That's my band. That's *me* on guitar."

Bursting into laughter, I said, "I figured that! I'm messing with you. The guitar hooks are killer. I'm impressed. The writing is decent, but it needs more character. Every part, every second of each song should be a hook. They should be short, believable, dynamic, and engage the listener from the first second. The band needs to be iconic and have an urgency about them."

"What do you mean urgent and iconic?"

"I need to hear an iconic voice. All great artists are identifiable the minute you hear them on the radio. For example, we both can probably tell within three seconds any Queen, Metallica, or Korn song by the drum sound, the guitar tone, or the vocal tone. This demo doesn't have that. However, I will say I like the call-and-response hook concept between the rapper and singer. The call-and-response theme could be a great identifier if you can get the songs stronger. Otherwise you're competing with an industry flooded right now with rap-rock bands. You need to stand out more. Hit songs, great vocals, identifiable sound."

Brad nodded. "Thanks, man. We are constantly working on new songs."

"Great! That's critical. Never stop writing. My favorite song is that second one. Do you have any others?"

"Really? You like the second song? That's probably our least favorite," he laughed. "We're working on a new song called 'Rhinestone.' I'll play it for you when it's done."

"I look forward to it, buddy. Either way, I'd love to see your band sometime. Even if it's just to give you some shit," I teased.

"We haven't booked our first gig yet, but I'll let you know."

I could feel Brad's focus. He and I shared the same addiction to music, and it inspired me. I was impressed with his ability to combine a logical and diplomatic approach to a creative business. Unconsciously, I had cemented my decision to believe in Brad, and nothing would shake that conviction.

CHAPTER 4

FIRST SIP OF WHISKEY

A HEAVY BASS LINE WAS RIPPING THROUGH MY OFFICE LIKE a stampede of bulls when a cassette tape came flying through the air. This time I caught it.

"Ah, another Xero cassette," I said, looking at the creepy baby head on the cover.

"The new song I told you about, 'Rhinestone,' is on there. We got rid of the song you liked most," he laughed.

The track listing was:

01. Rhinestone
02. Reading My Eyes
03. Fuse
04. Stick 'n' Move

"Why would you get rid of one of the best songs on the demo?"

I picked up the cassette and listened through. The baby head was intriguing and an indication of the care and artistic vision the guys put into the band's message. When it was finished, we played it back again.

"You've put this together intelligently," I said. "A well-rounded demo of no more than five songs, best songs first, all the songs sound different but are clearly the same band, and all the songs can fit on the same album. The production is raw and unpolished, like a bedroom demo, but that's good because it leaves room for an A&R person's potential vision."

Brad eased into the chair opposite my desk. I tried to hold back a grin. I wasn't sure why I liked the demo so much. Maybe it was the fact that I felt a connection with Brad, and I wanted to take him under my wing.

"I love the lyrics and cinematic lines of 'Rhinestone,'" I told him. "They're annoyingly stuck in my head, probably for the rest of my life," I laughed. "The chemistry between you and the rapper is obvious. 'Rhinestone' shows a lot of improvement."

A week later, I was sitting down listening to a new band from Chicago called Disturbed when Brad walked in with an ear-to-ear smile and slammed a flyer down on my desk.

"It's official! We play our first show on November fourteenth," he said. "You're going to come, aren't you?"

"What? I can't hear you!" Turning down the volume on the stereo, I grabbed the flyer and shook my head. "Shoot, I have a date on the fourteenth. I'll catch the next show though."

"It would be great if you could make it. Blow off your date and come check us out," he laughed. "Oh, I forgot. It's rare that you get a girl to agree to hang out with you."

"Ah, you're a musician and a comedian."

The Friday afternoon of the show, Brad left my office and I wished him luck. From my office window I could see him walking down Sunset to the Whisky a Go Go, then unloading his gear with his band. I felt a tinge of guilt. He was right. I wanted to support Brad, so I cancelled my plans, grabbed a slice of pizza, and walked up to the box office.

"I should be on Xero's list," I said to the girl with a tattoo on her arm of Raggedy Ann being stabbed in the heart.

"We don't have a guest list for Xero," she said without looking up. "Ten dollars please."

"He's good," the bouncer interrupted, motioning me inside the venue. The room was pretty packed. They were opening for System of a Down, who had just signed with Rick Rubin, and SX-10, which included Sen Dog from Cypress Hill. Los Angeles had a new scene developing right under our noses with System, Incubus, Static-X, Snot, Hoobastank, and others.

I scoped out the primarily twenty-one-to-twenty-seven-year-old male-dominated attendees, all in baggy pants hanging down past their asses, like Brad. My image clearly didn't fit in, so I pulled my tight jeans as low as they'd go until I could barely move. My sneakers squeaked against the sticky floor, and the room had the stench of sour beer mixed with a bit of Lysol—just like every rock club around the country. It smelled like rock and roll lived here.

I came in just as Xero walked on stage. I felt butterflies. No one knew who the band was. No one seemed to care. Brad, with his guitar slung low, headphones atop his curly hair, riffed on his guitar as the skilled rapper and vocalist each moved around the stage, along with the DJ who seemed to be more of an active musical participant than the token DJs used as props in most rap-rock bands. I had never met the guys, but somehow I connected with them. It was raw and energetic, the rapper was engaging, and the band seemed to be having fun. I was drawn in until someone next to me snickered and said, "That rapper looks like a smurf." At that point I realized he was wearing a white beanie, blue glasses, and white gloves. *Shit,* I thought. *He does kind of look like a smurf.* I refocused my thoughts on the band.

After about two minutes, people started talking to each other and lost interest in the guys pouring their hearts out in front of them. I made some quick notes on a napkin. "Vocals off key. Awkward stage presence. Decent songs. Didn't connect with the audience." With the last song playing, I scratched out some final thoughts and scribbled, "Potential!"

As I stuffed the napkin into my pocket, a kid to the side of me leaned over my shoulder. "You're taking notes on this band? You forgot to write down 'they sucked.'"

"Man, come on. You have no idea how hard it is up there, and that was their first show," I said, defending the band.

"Are you an A&R guy?" he replied.

"Well, kind of. I want to be. I'm a publisher with Zomba."

"Zomba? Never heard of it. I work at Columbia Records as an A&R assistant. I wouldn't waste your time on these guys. Xero? That about describes them."

"Thanks for your advice. My intern's the guitarist. I just came out to support, but I'll make up my own mind." I took it personally but then realized that an A&R person's job is to make immediate judgments. Still, I muttered, "What a dick," as I walked upstairs toward the dressing rooms.

Brad greeted me nodding his head, "You made it. I thought I saw you in the audience. Hey, guys. This is my boss, Jeff," Brad said to the band, who were all covered in sweat.

"Thanks for coming down," the rapper said with a smile. "My name's Mike. Nice to meet you."

"Nice to meet you all. Great set, by the way. I really like that song 'Rhinestone,'" I said as the other bands crammed into the green room and music blared around us. "Just wanted to say hi. Maybe we can talk later, in a more quiet, less sweaty-odor-filled room," I yelled. "I'll let you guys clean up."

"See you on Monday," Brad screamed back.

Brad arrived earlier than usual the following Monday morning. Throwing his Adidas jacket on the sofa, he planted himself down in front of my desk. "So, what'd you really think?"

"Look, man, it was great to see you live. You were awesome, and there's something there, but something is missing."

"Okay, do you have any constructive criticism?"

Glancing at my notes, I said, "The songs were good but could be better; the rapper was unique, had a cool vocal style; but the lead vocals were pitchy, to be honest. The band as a whole could be tighter, but you had fun, and that was evident. For a first gig, it's clear to me there's real potential. I'm seriously impressed."

"Is it cool if I bring the guys into the office? They'd love to talk to you."

"Of course. That's what I'm here for. I'd love to get to know them."

Two days later, Mark Wakefield, the lead singer, a tall, confident young man with an enigmatic and captivating presence, walked slowly down the hall. I held out my hand to shake his, and he nodded to me with his head held high, then reached out his hand to shake mine. Following him was Mike Shinoda, the rapper, who stopped and stared at a gold plaque for A Tribe Called Quest. He was quiet, absorbing everything going on around the office. He smiled politely and shook my hand, followed by bassist Dave Farrell, and drummer Rob Bourdon, who looked like a surfer. DJ Joe Hahn was quiet and reserved. Brad walked in last with a sense of pride as he waved to some of the Zomba employees. I knocked on a few office doors and introduced the band to a few execs. It was a full welcoming committee. Brad had already made a great impression on everyone at the company.

Sitting down in my office, my mind raced with intrigue as I listened to Mike's methodical, intelligent questions ping-ponging with Brad's intuitive remarks, culminating with the new song ideas Mike played for me, which he had recorded in his bedroom studio.

I hit the pause button on the tape deck. "Sorry to ask the obvious question," I started, "but how did you all meet?"

"I've known Mike since we were kids," said Brad. "We met Rob and Mark in high school in Agoura. I met Dave at UCLA, and Mike met Joe in art school." There was an interesting dynamic between Mark, Mike, and Brad. Each exuded different leadership qualities, and I wondered how they'd interact on a team level. Mark seemed to be the leader, but it was apparent from these first few minutes that Mike was more thoughtful and creative, and, ultimately, the quiet one in control. He didn't speak much, but when he did, his words had purpose. He was analytical, digesting everything I said along with the environment around him. We discussed music, the business of publishing, and record deals. I couldn't help but notice the ethnic and cultural diversity in the band. Mike was of Japanese heritage, and Joe was Korean. I was captivated on many levels.

"What are your musical influences? I know Brad is a diehard Metallica fan and gives me shit because I like *The Black Album,*" I laughed.

"You're not a real Metallica fan if your favorite record is *The Black Album.* Both *Master of Puppets* and *...And Justice for All* destroy *The Black Album.* Jeff's just into commercial hits," Brad laughed.

"Don't offend Brad's Metallica sensibilities," Mike smiled. "Have you heard of Styles of Beyond? I also love Wu-Tang and Depeche Mode. What about you?"

"I love everything from Queen, Nina Simone, Mary J., Zeppelin, Depeche Mode, STP, to Miles and Coltrane, the Bee Gees, '70s pop one-hit wonders, to George Michael, Tupac, Jay-Z, Dre, to KISS and Crüe. Even some country. As long as it has an identity, a sound, I can sing it, and it evokes an emotion or reaction in me," I said.

"You're all over the map. What did you think about us?" Mike asked.

His tone took me by surprise and made me feel like I was the one on stage, but his questions were direct and confident. "Considering I've seen your first and only show, I have a sense that there's something here. I think you and Brad have a chemistry that's intriguing, but it's very early. I need more time to give you real insight. Outside of that, I get that special feeling. You know the one when the hairs on your arm stand up and you get that funny tingling in your stomach?"

"I don't want to seem cynical, but how do you make decisions? What makes you able to decide who makes it and who doesn't have the talent?" Mike asked respectfully.

"I wonder that every day," I laughed. "I just have faith in myself to know when to have faith in others. There are certain undefinable qualities that I sense in artists that inspire me to invest time and energy into helping them reach their full potential. I have a strong sense of music, and when I'm at my best, I am able to find and bring out talent and qualities in people they didn't even know they had."

"How does that work?" Joe asked.

"I can see the light at the end of the tunnel, and I can direct you there, but I can't force you to it. For that relationship to work, it requires trust and communication. That doesn't mean that the artist and I will always see eye to eye, or always get along. The ability to argue over something is good if it pushes the artist to do better. Music consumes me like a beast. I want success for the artist so bad that when someone's full potential isn't being reached, it emotionally and physically stresses me out."

"Like Doctor Jekyll and Mister Hyde?"

"Just like that," I laughed. "Sometimes I'm a hard-ass and will drive you to the brink of thinking you want to kill me. The artist almost always thinks they're functioning at their top ability. In a band, there are various personalities, and not everyone is functioning at the same level at the same time. I will see the best attributes in you and let you know when you aren't doing your best work even when you may believe you're giving your all. You know when you're running up a hill and you think you're convinced you're going to collapse and die? Well, that's your brain simply flashing a warning signal, protecting you. Your body actually has an extra ten percent more to go before collapsing. Be prepared, because I will push you that full extra nine percent before you truly die—or kill me in the process. That will make the difference between the stars and the failures. But again, I can't do it alone."

"So, you may be interested in working with us?" Mark asked, lying back in his seat, one leg sprawled out while his back reclined, clearly trying to be the one in command.

"If you're interested after all the horrible warnings I just gave you about how hardcore I can be, you must be a brave soul. Developing a band is a ton of work, but I could be down with that. Let me sit with the idea," I said.

Brad laughed and pulled out a box. "Before we leave, happy birthday."

I opened the top to reveal a pair of new Adidas sweats.

"If you're going to be hanging with us, you need to look the part," he said. "The Nikes-and-Gap-jeans combo isn't cool." Hugging the band goodbye, I invited them to my birthday party that weekend. I knew I was about to sign these guys, and I realized I would have to revamp my wardrobe in the process.

CHAPTER 5

YOU WANNA SIGN YOUR INTERN?

MY ATTORNEY AND GOOD FRIEND DANNY HAYES TOSSED HIS surfboard into my beat-up 4Runner as I cranked Xero's demo loud enough to wake the sleepy beach town of Venice. "What are we listening to so deafeningly loud at seven in the morning?" Danny screamed as we drove along the coast looking for a great surf break.

"I can't stop listening to this demo," I yelled back. "This is my intern's band. I think there's something here."

We parked at El Porto beach, donning our full wetsuits, surveying the faces of the waves as the demo continued to blast through the speakers, providing the perfect soundtrack for our morning surf.

"Good shit, right?"

"The waves, yes. The band, I'm not sure."

Paddling through the white water, I said, "I think Xero has something special. We should develop this band."

"We?"

"Yeah. You and me together."

"Didn't you just tell me the band has only played one show? The demo sounds cool, but shouldn't you focus on getting Macy a deal?" he yelled over the waves. "I don't think it's smart to take on *two* development artists. Do you really believe in this particular band that much?"

"I just have a feeling about this band. And I love getting in on the ground floor and doing something meaningful. Anyone can come in after the hard work has been done. Where's the satisfaction in that?"

"The satisfaction is keeping your job. There's no rush, man. Don't let your ego make mistakes."

"It's definitely not ego. I may be ambitious and overly driven," I laughed, "but my passion is based in reality." I shook my head. "You and I only have a brief window of time to make an impact, and the clock is ticking. We are in our mid-twenties. This is our time." I slapped the surfboard in the water with my frozen hand. "If we don't have monumental success in the next couple years, we're fucked. By the time we're thirty, we'll be dinosaurs in the music industry. The time is now. I feel it."

"I can't feel anything right now, this water's so cold," Danny said as the saltwater mist from our last set of waves sprayed our faces. "You're like a football coach. But I feel like a solider being sent into war. We're surfing in Santa Monica, not in battle."

"This is a battle, Danny. Our competition is everyone else. We are fighting time. And we need to win. I'd love you to be the attorney on this. Be my wingman. This is going to be my priority."

"All right, let's do it. I can tell you'll never stop pushing unless I agree. But no matter what I think, it'll take a miracle to get Richard to approve a deal with your *intern*."

YOU WANNA SIGN YOUR INTERN?

"Let's do something so low-budget that he can't say no." As we waited for the next wave, I added imaginary figures in the air. "Four grand upon signing the publishing deal, a thousand-dollar demo budget, another ten grand if and when we sign the band to a major label, and then like another twenty when the album is released on a major."

"Forty grand in total? I just did a deal for a half mil. A four grand advance is nothing. Richard can't say no to that. And that's a great deal for a band that's played only one show. If this band is successful, it will be the first contract negotiated on surfboards," he laughed. "More importantly, I'm starving and in desperate need of some tacos! You're buying lunch."

"You got it. I'm gonna make this four grand the best investment ever. After lunch I'm going home and putting together a deal memo."

"Sounds like an awesome weekend," Danny scoffed.

On Monday, December 1, 1997, at 9:00 a.m., I faxed the Xero development deal memo, outlining all the legalities and contractual points that I had worked on over the weekend and FedExed the demo tape to the New York office.

My boss, Richard Blackstone, called me the following day. "I saw your fax, and I listened to the demo along with some of the other A&R people at Jive. Personally, I think it's good, but no one here really hears what's so special about this band. You know, your job depends on your ability to make us money, not on losing it."

"Oh, shit...I'm supposed to make *you* money? I was so confused. Is this a for-profit business?" I said sarcastically. "I'm gonna make you so much money you can take a bath in it. Imagine it now."

"Jeff, don't ever imagine me taking a bath," he laughed. "You're such a salesperson."

"Isn't that part of my job? Selling the vision?" I replied.

"Just to be clear, you want to sign your *intern* to a co-pub deal? And they've only played one show? I know the deal you proposed is unbelievably risk free for us and very reasonable. But you want me to give money to this kid who is supposed to be working *for you*? Shouldn't he be helping you develop your *other* artists such as Macy Gray, who you convinced me to sign not too long ago and still doesn't have a label deal? It's your job not only to tell us the deals that we should do, but the deals we shouldn't. Let the other publishers do the risky deals. I need you focusing on our signed artists and writers. We are heavily invested in these artists."

"Richard, I can do it all. I'm an OCD multitasker. Plus, a four-thousand-dollar advance is virtually nothing! If I don't get Macy or Xero a deal in one year you can take Xero's advance out of my salary. Please trust me!"

"I'm not going to put that pressure on you because I know you put it on yourself. I trust you. Plus, you don't make enough salary," he laughed. "If you can convince the band to do a four-thou-sand-dollar advance, then I guess we can't get hurt."

"Thanks. You're the best boss in the world."

"Well, you're a great salesperson. Remember to get Macy a deal too!"

Two days later, Richard sent Danny Hayes and me the Xero deal memo. Carrying the agreement into my office like a newborn infant, careful not to crease any pages, I set them on my desk and waited to surprise Brad. I had discussed with the band the previous weekend that I was going to try to get them a development deal, and they were all excited about the possibility of working together.

"Buddy, we are going to do this!" I blurted out as Brad entered. I stood and gave him a high five.

"Do what? What are we high-fiving for?"

"I got you a development deal!" I said, expecting an amazing reaction.

He was silent and smiled. "Okay." He fidgeted around in his seat.

"Just okay? I thought you'd be doing cartwheels and jumping off the walls. Artists struggle for years before being offered a contract like this. This never happens."

"Cool. It's good news," he said.

"Hell yeah, it's *great* news! You've just achieved something awesome. Congrats! Let's go grab a Subway sandwich and celebrate! I just put my job on the line for the band."

"I am excited, but you don't have to put your job on the line, man."

"Every choice I make is putting my job on the line. But I believe in you. I believe in the band."

We took our usual stroll down to the Sunset Boulevard Subway, where we slowly ate our turkey sandwiches and glanced over the contract for about thirty minutes without saying a word.

Finally, Brad spoke, still flipping the pages. "There's a lot in this contract I don't understand. It's Christmas vacation. I know you got a lot going on with Macy. Give me some time, and we can sign this first thing in January."

The footlong turkey stuck in my stomach like a lead balloon, as did Brad's tepid reaction.

CHAPTER 6

REINVENTING MACY'S PARADE

It was Christmas time and Macy Gray was like an angel with broken wings. Darryl Swann, Macy's producer, and Jeremy Ruzumna, Macy's keyboardist, met with Macy and me at Paramount studios to work on her new demos..

We were sitting in the lounge, when Macy got up to go to the restroom. Her journal fell to the floor. I leaned over to pick it up, and it opened to an account of her raw and dramatic past.

That evening we grabbed drinks. I said, "Hey, something is on my mind, and I feel horrible about it, but I'm torn...."

"You're not dropping me, are you?" she asked. "I know this isn't going the way you want things to go."

"No, no, nothing like that. I absolutely love your voice, but I did something unintentionally that I am not proud of." Looking up at me from the side of her eyes, she waited for what was next. "Look,

I'm sorry, but I accidentally saw something really emotional and personal in your diary."

"You read my diary?"

"No, I didn't *read* it, but it was open and I glanced at one page. What I saw was really emotional, and I'm sorry for what you've gone through." She appeared more embarrassed than angry. I continued. "Please capture what's in that diary, the deep place in your heart, and express your feelings about hope and reality. I'm sure your distress will resonate with people."

"Damn. I don't know what to feel, or really say."

"All I can tell you is that I can relate. It's easy to appear strong on the outside, but inside we are all fragile and vulnerable. I think all of us put on a show for the outside world. Especially artists. Everyone has demons. Good artists find a way of expressing those demons that the rest of the world can relate to, and that takes courage. My biological father left when I was one year old, and, later, he committed suicide. I carry around a fear of abandonment and failure. You have the ability to inspire others to make it through the dark times."

Pausing and holding her drink, she looked up and nodded at me. "You're cool. A little crazy, but cool. Just don't look through my diary anymore. I don't want you to get any darker," she said.

The next day, something extraordinary was happening. Macy was singing brilliant, inspiring melodies that melted my heart so much that tears welled in my eyes. In awe, I quickly invited a few A&R friends over to the office to listen to the rough demos as soon as they were finished. I allowed Brad to sit in on the meetings so he could get an education in pitching music.

The A&R execs were blown away, but upon telling them it was Macy Gray, in unison they all put their hands up as if to say, "Uh, no, not Macy. We've seen her live before. Pass."

I realized that I had to rebrand Macy if I was ever going to get her a record deal. A new sound should mean a new name.

"Actually, I had a band years before I met you called Mushroom," she said.

Her new temporary name was born. Brad and I made cassette copies of the Mushroom demo and FedExed them to Atlantic, Reprise, Virgin, Arista, and Polly Anthony at Epic. The comments from this test group of respected executives would serve as a guide for the changes I would need to make to the arrangement and mix. Then I would amend the shopping process accordingly.

"Don't you think changing the name of an artist is misleading?" Brad asked.

"It depends on the way you look at it. I will do whatever it takes to get people to listen to this with a fresh, unbiased mind. Macy has an iconic voice that needs to be heard. By the way, how's our contract going?" I asked.

"It's going, man. Give us some time. But when we shop our music, we'll get a deal because our music is real from the start. Just don't make us change our name," he said with a smile.

"Don't give me a reason to!" I jokingly replied.

CHAPTER 7

THOSE GUYS LOOK IMPORTANT

ACK AT THE OFFICE, BRAD AND I WERE LISTENING TO DEMOS as I was mailing Mushroom cassettes to A&R people. I looked at Brad, who was hard at work.

"You should come play poker with me and my friends," I told him. "Lee, the guy I was in a band with, and some other attorneys will be there. My girlfriend, Carmen, is bringing over some food. It will be fun."

"I don't know how to play poker. And most of those guys are out of my league," he replied.

"You're smarter than most of the attorneys there, so you can probably clean up big time. I'll teach you how to play."

"Didn't you say you have a roommate?"

"Yeah. It's my dad's buddy. I live in his condo. He's like twice my age but super cool. His stepson is part of the Dust Brothers."

"The who Brothers?"

"The Dust Brothers. My roommate's son is Mike Simpson. He produced albums from the Beastie Boys, Beck, and Hanson. In fact, he just produced some songs for the new Rolling Stones album and does A&R at DreamWorks. I'll send your demo over to him. He may come to see Macy next week as well."

The following day I sent the Xero demo to Mike Simpson, who responded a few days later.

"Hey, Jeff. I gotta tell you, I like the Mushroom vibe."

"What did you think about the Xero cassette?"

"That's a different story. I think that needs a lot more work, but I can see you working some magic with them in the future. My stepdad said he met Brad at the poker game last night."

"Yeah, he wiped us out. Beginner's luck."

"Maybe you just suck at poker," he laughed.

"That, too. But I have a feeling Xero is gonna be big. I'll send you songs as they progress. Thanks, buddy."

The following week I brought Brad to Luna Park in West Hollywood to witness a huge showcase for Macy. I went to the bar and handed Brad a Heineken.

"Thanks, but I'll just have water," he said. "I don't drink. I actually haven't ever had a beer before."

"Good for you. Leaves more for me," I replied. He stood next to me and Carmen, watching the people file in through the venue door. This showcase was a make-or-break moment for my young career.

"Those guys look important," Brad said, pointing at two different people.

"How can you tell?"

"You have that smile I see when you're part nervous, part excited."

"That's Clive Davis and Jimmy Iovine. They're definitely important. They're legends. There's Polly Anthony from Epic, too."

Just then, Jason Flom walked up. "Jeff, good to see you. I thought I'd check out Macy live," he said.

"Jason, let me introduce you to my girlfriend, Carmen, and Brad, my intern. He's in an awesome band called Xero."

"Hey, Brad. I'd love to hear your music sometime."

After Jason walked away, Carmen smiled and said, "Brad, you should come over for dinner. Have the rest of the band come over to eat before you play."

"Your girlfriend's really nice," Brad whispered in my ear. "By the way, I appreciate you including me on everything."

"Of course. That's the only way you'll learn."

Just then, Macy came over to say hi. "Hey, Jeff played me your demo. Really cool stuff," she said to Brad.

"Thanks so much, and good luck tonight," Brad responded. "I love the energy in this room. I know someday soon we're going to showcase for labels like this. Just wait," he added, leaning into me.

"Oh, I'm waiting, buddy. I love your confidence."

I watched Brad walk the room. He was absorbing everything around him. I was impressed with his body language, and his easy communication with the execs. This kid was quickly picking up nuances of the business and I was proud to be his mentor.

The showcase was a game changer. Macy's performance was so genuine, and the songs so powerful, that a bidding war ensued among all the major labels. Interscope offered to buy her a house while Epic bought her a brand-new Escalade just to entice her to sign. The Escalade and the magnanimous Polly Anthony won her over, and she signed to Epic—and then changed her stage name back to Macy Gray.

The rebranding worked, and my passion and confidence for developing talent increased.

CHAPTER 8

INVISIBLE INK

RICHARD BLACKSTONE CALLED. "CONGRATS ON MACY," HE said. "I want to follow up on your intern's band. You had us get this contract ready for you over seven months ago. Why is it taking so long?"

"Thanks. I appreciate you believing in the band. As to why they haven't signed, I'll find out. Actually, guess who just walked into my office? I'll call you back."

"Whew, it's hot out there," Brad said, pulling up his baggy shorts.

With Richard's voice in my head, I went straight to the matter at hand. "Brad, I'm a little confused. It's been seven months, and you keep avoiding what's going on with the publishing offer. This is getting ridiculous."

"The guys just aren't sure it's the right move, like, what the benefit will be."

"Brad, where is this coming from? You aren't shopping my deal, are you?"

"No, of course not."

"Well then get the guys in here again, and let's make this work, so we can get on the fast track to getting Xero a record deal. I love you guys. Let's do this!"

Bowing his head and placing his hands together, he said, "I'll talk to the guys again. Thanks for being patient."

A few days later, I was speaking with a young manager who had called the office. "I'm Adrian Miller. I think we met through DJ Lethal. I've been kinda helping manage Xero. They came to me with a publishing deal you offered them."

"Wait up, you're managing the band? They never told me anything about this. I'm confused."

"I told them I didn't know enough about publishing and, honestly, there's a bit of a power struggle in the band."

"A power struggle? They've only played one show. How much struggle can there be?"

"Mark thinks he's the leader, when it's really Mike that does almost all the work. There's some internal band stuff, too. I think Mike is looking to work with other artists separate from the band. I know they were hoping to get a record deal first, but I think the band, especially Mark, feels you can help them."

I laughed, "They want a record deal after playing only one show? The minute we get the deal done we can start shopping for labels, but they're going to need better songs, press, and a good buzz. Anyways, please put in a good word. And thanks for the info."

Another three weeks went by when I ran into a buddy at the Whisky.

"Hey Jeff, I'm hearing good things about the new Korn album. How's it going with signing Xero?"

"Xero? How'd you know about that band?"

"Was I not supposed to know? I heard you made an offer on an unknown band called Xero. They're saying they have a publishing offer. I think they're speaking to a couple of managers, maybe a couple of publishers?"

"You've gotta be kidding me!"

"I don't know; I just heard some things floating around. I don't mean to start anything, so don't hold me to it. I thought you must have known."

I had no proof that the rumor was true, so I decided to speak to Brad in person.

The familiar head of curly hair popped into my office on Friday afternoon, smiling and happy. "Hey, Jeff," he said, sticking out his hand to fist bump mine, which was placed firmly on my desk.

"Sit down, man."

"Where's happy Blue? I have good news, man!"

"Happy Blue isn't so happy, Delson. What's the good news?"

"We agreed to do the publishing deal!"

"Oh, really?"

Whatever the reason for the sudden change of heart, the rumors didn't matter anymore. All that mattered was they'd be signing with Zomba. I decided to focus on the positive and immerse myself into making Xero the biggest band on the planet.

After nine months, the contract was finally being signed. The band and I decided to meet Danny Hayes at the law offices of Manatt, Phelps, & Phillips in West Los Angeles for the official signing. In honor of the occasion I purchased a pair of Levi's, two sizes too big, and we all walked the halls of the law firm, dressed in baggy jeans and T-shirts. One attorney was screaming on the phone, another was walking a client out, and another looked like he needed a drink. We met Danny's partner, Scott Harrington, and then we were handed six sets of documents with colored tabs earmarked for signatures. Mark, Mike, Brad, Joe, Rob, Danny, and I all signed the paperwork in the conference room and then decided to take a photo commemorating the deal on the roof of the building on a bright, beautiful, sunny California day. None of us had any idea of what the future would hold, but we all were young, alive, and in good spirits. Brad went from being my intern to my newly signed artist and a client. Not a bad internship! We were now working together on his future.

The following week I took Brad to the Mesa Boogie showroom on Sunset Boulevard. He explained that his signature sound is derived from his PRS guitar combined with the modern tone of the Mesa Dual Rectifier. He ordered the Rectifier head, and we left feeling things were finally on their way.

The first course of action was to get into the studio and record some hits. I sent out the initial Xero demo to over a dozen top rock producers and received over a dozen passes. I finally convinced Macy's producer, Darryl Swann, to jump on board, negotiating a four-song demo for $1,000. Darryl had been instrumental in getting Macy's sound so I thought he'd be able to help Xero as well. We scheduled our recording session for August 25, 1998.

One evening before we started recording, I was fortunate enough to meet Brad's father, Don Delson. Don was as calm and collected as his son, and he wanted to make sure Brad's career was in the right hands. I was deeply inspired by his belief in his son and was determined to prove to Brad's family, my family, and Zomba that Xero would be the band of a lifetime. When I got home, I called my father.

"Dad, I just spoke to this kid's father I'm working with, and he is really encouraging his son. This kid went to UCLA, too. He's smart."

"Jeff, I get you enjoy what you're doing, but music is a hobby, not a career. You have a law degree. That's a career. Music is a hard and uncaring business and you're only as good as your last success."

"I wish you understood; Brad's dad really supports him and understands that music is a legitimate career. The point of this call was to connect on some level. I'll prove it to you. The more you doubt me the more it fuels me, Dad."

"Well, then at least I'm doing something right," he said. "Brad's father has entrusted you with his son's career, and you need to keep your word to him."

With my dad's sentiments in mind, the next morning, Darryl, the members of Xero, and I opened the massive doors and stepped into Paramount Recording Studio on Santa Monica Boulevard. "Wow, by the smell of these halls and all the legendary plaques on the walls, you can imagine just who had recorded hits here while pacing the walkways," Mark said with a nervous tinge in his voice.

"It's inspiring, right?" I replied as he nodded, holding his head high.

The band stepped up to the heavy studio door to the big tracking room in Studio C.

"Are you familiar with Pro Tools?" I asked Darryl, leaning over the console.

"Not that much. We are going to go all analog on this," he replied as he helped Mike with some beats on the Akai MPC.

Darryl bought used two-inch reels with the advance money and sliced all the leader tape out of it so we had a solid tape. He striped the tape with SMPTE time code. From there he had to create the structure, count bars to leave gaps for empty spaces for the live drums and record the drum machine in certain spots, print it, and then record live drums for the spots later. After all the musical tracks were laid down, it was time for vocals. Dressed in an XL white T-shirt, Mark sang his guts out in the vocal booth, but that special "something" was missing, and Mark knew it. "Can I talk to Brad and Mike?" he said into the mic. "In private."

After a few minutes, Mike came out into the recording bay. "Mark is a bit stressed out. If everyone could leave the studio while Mark records, that'd be great."

The band members proceeded to leave the room, and Darryl and I sat at the console. Swiveling in my impressive-looking Herman Miller studio chair, Mike looked at me and said, "Sorry, Mark meant you too, Jeff." I was stunned, having never been asked to leave the studio during a session that I had set up.

"You want *me* to leave?"

"Brad and I can handle this," Mike said confidently.

I joined the rest of the band in the lobby. After a few hours, Daryl poked his head out of the recording booth and motioned me to meet him outside. "Your boy is struggling. He's super gun-shy and needs a lot of space and privacy."

"I'm sure he's just warming up. Give him a minute."

"It's been a couple hours, and I'm afraid he's not getting better. Either way, we'll make the demo sound as good as possible."

"I appreciate it, Daryl. I just want to make sure the songs are great and the vocals are the best they can be. You were instrumental with Macy, so let's get that positive vibe!"

"I agree. I'll get Mark's vocals sounding awesome. Just be aware, I kind of sense a power struggle between Mike and Mark."

"That's interesting you see that, too. You'd figure the head of the band would be the lead vocalist, but Mike is a natural leader and the guys all respect him. Defer to Mike. We've got to allow his vision to be authentic. If you or I don't feel the songs are there, then we can step in."

CHAPTER 9

THE LAST RESORT

Throughout September, Brad and I sent out Xero's demos. I invited every label I could get on the phone to see the band showcase at their rehearsal space. The reaction was lukewarm, with just one person expressing interest in the band's potential. His name was Danny Goodwin. He was credited with signing Culture Club, an iconic '80s group with a phenomenal lead vocalist in Boy George. Other than Goodwin, I received mild interest from Michelle Ozbourn at Arista. The outlook was dismal.

The band would come in with new music every week or so. One day, Mike and Joe handed me an Urban Network Compilation CD titled *Rapology 14*. "Our song 'Fiends' is on there, and I created the artwork," Mike said. "Joe's working at the promo company and I'm also working with Styles of Beyond on some tracks."

"Congrats! You gave me some of Styles of Beyond music before," I said, impressed with Mike's drive and talent. "You're doing everything right. Keep the connections and doing anything and everything you can do to broaden the scope of your music and expose Xero to the world."

Brad and I became closer as he joined my friends and me for my bachelor party and attended my wedding to Carmen on September 28, 1998. My father came over to Brad at the reception, as Macy Gray and the band performed on the dance floor. "My son says wonderful things about you. He always keeps his word, and he's assured me that he won't stop until he's made sure you're in a secure career."

It was a Monday evening in October when I stepped into the Troubadour to see a band my friend Brett Bair kept telling me about. There was some unsettling energy in the demos, so I was intrigued enough to see the band live.

As I entered the Troubadour I took in the scent. It had a more woodsy smell than the Roxy or Whisky with a little bit more finesse and a more intimate setting. I grabbed a beer, and looked around. I only spotted one A&R person in attendance. I had heard this band had been passed on many times, but I wanted to give them a shot.

The lead singer with black spiked hair got on stage, took the mic in his hands like he was going to murder someone, and the band lit up. The singer had a clear identity, and his stage presence was engaging. He did a sort of shuffle that I wasn't sure I liked, but he owned it. I didn't hear a hit song, but I felt the band was further along than Xero. The second song ended, and the singer said, "Thanks, we're Papa Roach from Sacramento."

Weird name, but so was Limp Bizkit. Everything I saw, everything I heard, was processed in my mind as a comparison to Xero. Watching this band and their charismatic vocalist, I realized Xero was missing a strong lead singer.

I greeted the band after the show.

"Hey, Jeff, thanks for coming down. I'm Jacoby," the lead singer said.

"You guys should come by the office tomorrow. I really liked the show, and we should talk."

I entered the office the following morning and called Brad at home. "Brad, I saw a great live band last night at the Troubadour. They're kind of your competition."

"Which band?"

"Papa Roach. They'll be in the office today. You should check out the demo."

"I can't make it to the office, but let me know how it goes."

That afternoon, Jacoby, Dave, Tobin, and Jerry, with their manager, Brett Bair, walked into my office. They seemed a little like Xero: young and inexperienced, but Jacoby commanded the room. There was an urgency about him. We listened to their songs, "Revenge," "Snakes," and "Legacy."

I sat back in my chair and thought, *Is this better than the Xero demos?* The answer was no.

"I like the demo. How close are you to signing a major-label deal?"

"Labels have come to check us out, but nothing certain yet," Brett said.

"There's two issues. First, I have a rock band that I'm developing and trying to get a deal for right now, too. Second issue is that I think you're in the same boat as my other band. You both need a single, or three."

I was itching to get their opinion on Xero. They were a captive audience, and I could gauge their reaction. "Here, let me know what you think," I said as I reached over and grabbed the Xero CD. "Rhinestone" blasted out of my speakers at a higher volume than I played Roach's demo. The band shrunk a bit in their seats. This was Papa Roach's meeting, and I was pitching them Xero when they were hoping I'd want to sign them. I felt like an asshole.

"That's pretty cool," Jacoby said. "Are they close to a deal?"

"Well, that's the problem. I think they're great, but it's been really tough to get a label to· commit. But I think they're onto something."

"Yeah, that element of electronic, with guitar-driven hard edge riffs. That's tight. The rapper has a cool flow, and the music seems authentic."

"I'd love for you guys to do some shows together."

"Yeah, we're getting a pretty good following, coming out here almost every week from Sacto. We'd love to be signed to Zomba with them. What's the name of the band?"

"They're called Xero. I'm not sure I can take on another similar development deal for a rock band without it being signed to a major a label. My boss would kill me. He keeps saying I need to *make* money for the publishing company instead of spending it. That just sounds so selfish." I laughed.

Coby was clearly disappointed. "Well, we're hungry. Your band Xero sounds like our competition," he said, only somewhat jokingly. "I'd love to meet them."

CHAPTER 10

THE OTHER TWO PERCENT

ONCE THE DEMOS WERE FINISHED, I SENT THEM OUT TO every label possible. The band's enthusiasm was in full swing as Mark booked a Halloween gig at a fraternity in Long Beach. Danny Hayes and I brought out Danny Goodwin, VP of A&R from Virgin Records. On the ride down, we blasted the demo until Goodwin was so pumped by our faith in the band that he was almost ready to sign them before he stepped out of my truck.

Students walked around with beer-filled red Solo cups as the band prepared to perform, dressed up as characters from the film *Dead Presidents*.

Danny pointed out, "The band hasn't touched the beers I put up on stage for them."

"Yeah, they're not really into partying. They're focused on the music. That's what's important."

THE OTHER TWO PERCENT

After a decent start, things started to wane during their third song, and the crowd began to dissipate.

Goodwin looked concerned. "What's with the vocalist? He's really pitchy."

"It's the monitors. He can't hear himself. It's a fraternity show."

"He'll be better if I bring the heads of Virgin down, won't he?" Goodwin asked.

"Of course. Don't worry," Danny assured him, before whispering to me, "Jeff, you gotta get Mark stronger or we're in deep shit. Like up to here," he said pointing to his forehead.

A few weeks later Xero performed at a UCLA fraternity. I invited my friend Steve, who worked in radio promotion and was always one to give solid, constructive criticism. Within four minutes Steve leaned over to me, "Bro, your band just cleared a party with a free keg. That's hard to do."

Most bands would have been upset, blaming outside elements or the wrong crowd, but Xero didn't let the negative reactions get them down. The band seemed more determined than ever to make their sound known. In my life, I've seen rejection have two effects on people. It will break their spirit, or it will make them try harder. At the end of the day, 98 percent give up. The remaining 2 percent were like Xero...and me.

The band started dropping off cassette demos up and down the famed hipster area of Melrose Avenue, and I finally booked a couple small gigs with my friend Mike Galaxy, a small local promoter who was passionate about discovering new artists. All the A&R reps that came to see Xero passed, usually walking out by the third song.

September and October were marked by uneventful record label meetings and failed showcases. Just when it seemed all hope was lost, I received two promising calls on November 4, 1998. One was from Matt Aberle at Reprise/Warner, who wanted to set up a showcase for Xero on November 14. The other call was from David Simone and Eddie Rosenblatt, the president and CEO of Geffen Records, to whom I hadn't even sent the disc, but who invited me to come to their offices that afternoon.

I walked a block up to the Geffen offices on Sunset, eager to know the reason for the meeting.

"We missed the boat on Macy Gray," David Simone said. "If you had the ability to sign someone right now, who would it be?"

Pulling the Xero 818 demo out of my leather jacket, I handed it to him. He placed the CD in the player and listened without interruption. My hands gripped the sides of the chair as I braced myself for the oncoming impact of rejection, and the inevitable sound of the eject button, but David left the CD in the player, and looked at Eddie. "Interesting. What makes you believe this is different than all the other rap rock out there?"

"Aside from the unique blend of hip hop and rock, the individual members are different. I know this sounds weird, but the guitar player really thinks about what he says and does, like he analyzes the effect of each sentence before the words leave his mouth. The DJ integrates the turntable as a percussive, melodic instrument, as opposed to ear candy, actually using guitar pedals so the sounds all blend together seamlessly. The rapper's lyrical style is intense and cinematic, not about girls and money, but internal struggles and overcoming adversity. It's a thinking person's band of amazing, intelligent artists, who run the band like a business. These guys aren't going to get drunk and destroy a hotel room. They're the ones that will end up owning the hotel."

"It's clear that you love the band," David said in his English accent. "I respect your belief and dedication to them. Eddie and I will discuss, but let's set up a dinner when I'm back from traveling in the next couple weeks."

THE OTHER TWO PERCENT

The meeting felt positive, but I didn't want to get the band's hopes up. Their focus had to be on the immediate Reprise/Warner showcase a week later. The guys hunkered down in the rehearsal room and worked on the live show.

On November 14, the band showcased for Matt Aberle from Reprise/Warner. The performance was average, but what impressed me about the band was their affability. Brad and Mike tried to interact with Matt after the show, asking him questions and looking him in the eye. I felt their personality salvaged the less-than-stellar performance.

Walking me outside to the parking lot, Matt said, "I like the guys. The singer needs some work. The entire band does, actually, but there may be something there."

"The band has what it takes. Tonight was a little off, but I assure you they'll be getting a deal shortly."

"If you can get the band stronger, I'll bring down David Kahne. We have something scheduled on the twenty-third, and I think we can stop by after."

Matt left, and I walked back into the rehearsal room. Mike nodded to me and asked what Matt thought.

"On the twenty-third, he's going to bring down his boss, David. He produced Sublime, The Bangles, Sugar Ray. He's a legend."

"We could have done better," Mike said. "I can see it in your eyes. We know we need some work."

"I really appreciate you realizing that. That's part of being a success. Knowing when there's room for improvement and not making excuses. Is there any way you can give me some insight into the songs you write? It will help me get to know you more as an artist and help my pitch to labels."

"Sure," he said. "I also have a couple new tracks I want to get your opinion on. I'll drop them off this week."

CHAPTER 11

IT'S ALL HAPPENING

On Tuesday, November 17, Mike knocked on my office door.

"Happy birthday, Jeff! Got you a special present." He dropped a stack of seven pages on my desk along with a CD. "You asked for the lyrics. I also gave you a bit of the inspiration behind the songs."

"Wow. Thanks."

"Are you really going to read it?"

"Of course. This is way more than I could have asked for, so I appreciate the time you spent on it."

Mike waved goodbye. When all was quiet, after the janitorial staff had left for the evening, under the neon glow of the lights flickering outside on the boulevard, I blasted Mike's music while reading the lyrics and processing his introspective notes. For the first time, I was allowed an intimate glimpse into his musical mind.

First was "Rhinestone," from the band's original demo. The song was written during the transition from high school to college. Mike's notes expressed frustration with feeling helpless and indicated the song was about grappling with an individual's insignificance in a world that seemed so big and intimidating, with so many issues that almost nothing could ever be corrected. He mentioned that the lyrics attempt to reconcile paranoia, anger, blaming others, and the naivete that comes when one has to see the world for what it is.

I bit my lip in excitement. I felt very connected to Mike at that moment.

"Esaul," "Pictureboard," "Fiends," "Stick 'n' Move," "Carousel," and "Slip." I listened with a fervor that sent my mind racing. I knew these songs by heart, but looking at the lyrics and meaning behind them elicited a vision of Mike performing his art in an arena. Next was "p o i n t i l l i s m," which was something Mike was creating for a soundtrack. His description was that he felt very alone while writing the song during the transitional period when he started concentrating on music. He'd just gotten a new job and was spread so thin that he didn't have time to hang out with his friends. He wrote that he needs to work hard, or sacrifice, in order to succeed. He had crossed out that last sentence in his notes. I wanted to know what he was thinking. What I did know, was that Mike was intense, driven, and focused.

Mike's verses on "Slip" were intoxicating. His talent was on full display as the pre-chorus flowed seamlessly into a slightly underwhelming chorus. But his brilliant vocal interplay with Brad's guitar in the first half of the intense bridge leading into a cathartic and beautiful release made this one of my favorites.

Brad's guitar line in "Esaul" felt iconic. The back and forth with Joe on the turntables reminded me of a western movie duel. This was already one of my favorites during rehearsals. I then flipped the page to "Carousel." He wrote that the song deals with the patterns of behavior associated with denial and the inability to deal with personal problems. The last two lines in the song he wrote from the standpoint of the interchange between a problem and the solution.

"Step Up" was written in response to the trend of sticking hip hop into heavy alternative music in a careless way. Mike felt that artists should strive to represent themselves and their music with authenticity, originality, and respect for hip hop. He went on to write that he didn't consider himself a hip hop expert but the band needed to push themselves harder than they were, because hip hop was not a moniker to be thrown into a song for the sake of street credibility. I felt a newfound respect for Mike's artistic integrity.

At eight o'clock that night I called Matt Aberle's cell and he picked up.

"Matt, this band Xero is going to be massive. Trust me on this. Get David Kahne out ASAP."

A couple of days later, I sat with the band in the rehearsal room. "This is a big opportunity, guys. David Kahne is head of A&R for Warner/Reprise. He can pull the trigger and sign an artist, so everything needs to be on point. Play like your lives depend on it."

The band assured me they were confident in their ability to crush the showcase, and I had faith in them to do so.

Brad and Dave Farrell came over to my house on Saturday, November 21, to celebrate my birthday, and the following day, the band left their blood and sweat on the Leeds Rehearsal showcase stage for David Kahne, but David wasn't impressed.

"I'm just not seeing what Matt or you see. There's no real star there. But nice meeting you finally. I've heard your name quite a bit," Kahne said as he shook my hand goodbye. I reentered the rehearsal room, head hung low by the all-too-familiar sting of rejection.

Mike threw up his hands, and the band shook their heads. "What the hell do these guys need to see?"

"We killed that showcase!" Mark said, frustrated.

"I agree, but A&R is totally subjective. David's a brilliant guy, so maybe we're missing something. Either way, I feel your pain."

That afternoon, I returned to my Zomba office feeling defeated. I slumped in my chair and bathed in silence. The phone rang. It was David Simone at Geffen. "You have time for dinner?" he asked me, encouragingly. "Meet me at Dan Tana's on Santa Monica."

An hour later, we ordered steaks, and I waited with as much patience as I could muster, dying to find out what his thoughts were.

Finally, I spoke. "So, what did you and Eddie think about the Xero demo?"

Taking a bite of his salad and wiping his mouth, David said, "We like it a lot. I can hear why you believe in them. They just need an A&R person who sees the vision."

I sat in utter silence waiting for him to finish the sentence. He kept me hanging while he took another bite of salad. This was followed by a long sip of water. *Please finish the conversation with something positive*, I thought. "So...?"

"So, we were not only impressed by the demo, but by you as well. We're going to clean house in the A&R department, and we'd like to offer you a position. Depending on how this works out, we'd be willing to have you make Xero your first signing."

I was finally being offered an A&R job. I couldn't contain my excitement. "Wow. That's an honor. Thank you," I managed. "Do you need to see the band showcase?"

"We want you, and we want the band. I don't need to see them. I trust your judgment. But let's get your deal moving first. Eddie and I will get something over to Danny Hayes this week. It would be great to have you on the team."

I was so excited I went home and hugged my dogs. I was so afraid I would jinx the job offer by talking about it I kept it to myself, not even telling Carmen. It almost seemed too perfect and unrealistic. I called Danny Hayes the next morning. "Hey, buddy. Have you gotten any calls about me?"

"About you gaining weight since you've been married?" Danny replied sarcastically.

"What? No. Have I gained weight? I'm just checking to see if anyone called. Forget it. By the way, now I'm going on a diet."

Frustrated, I threw some new demos in the CD player, and the phone rang. "Dude, your ears must have been burning! Great news. Geffen wants you over there to do A&R. They're revamping, and they love you."

"That's why I was asking fifteen minutes ago. What about Xero? Are they making an offer for the band?"

"They want you to sign first before committing to the band. But this is great. Congrats!"

Barely able to contain my excitement, I called Brad and requested a band meeting to discuss Geffen. I didn't want to tell him over the phone. "I've got great news!"

"Awesome. We have news, too. Let's all discuss in your office. We're excited," Brad said.

The next day the guys filed in, half the band sitting and half standing.

"Guys, who goes first?"

Brad said, "You called the meeting, so you go."

"Okay." I opened my hands as if to unveil a surprise. "Looks like I am going to do A&R for Geffen!"

"That's incredible!" Congrats and high-fives all around. "So you're going to be able to sign us?"

"They want to ink my deal first, but they love the demo and they're totally down to sign you, even without a showcase!"

"Geffen is amazing," Mike said, "but didn't you say Danny Goodwin at Virgin loved us? Couldn't we start a buzz with other major labels?"

The color drained from my face. "Well, Goodwin *likes* you guys but said the live show needs to improve, and leveraging the *potential* Geffen deal is a good move only if we have a huge fanbase, solid touring history, press, radio play, good merchandise sales, and some film and TV placements. Then, it would possibly motivate all the other major labels to jump in and make competing offers, but we sadly have none of these elements. Either way, Geffen loved the demos so we're golden!"

"We heard your good news," Mark said. "Our good news is we just booked a showcase for the eighteenth of December at the Whisky. You could invite all the labels down to see us play. Start a bidding war!"

Shaking my head, I said, "Don't do a big showcase. It's too risky. Trust me. There's a whole psychology to showcasing. I'm going to get Danny Hayes on speaker."

After explaining the band's plan, Danny blurted out a resounding, "No. No public showcase, guys."

"You have your publisher and attorney both saying it's a bad idea," I added. "The issue with an open showcase at a place like the Whisky is that the labels want to see: a) if you can draw fans and pack a room, b) the reaction from your fans, and more importantly, c) the reaction from the *non-fans* that were there to see another band. If the audience reaction is lukewarm or negative, then you're fucked. If multiple A&R people from different labels show up, either it can start a bidding war or word can spread that the band sucks. We've got Geffen already interested without a showcase. The risk-reward ratio is too high."

Danny added, "Plus, the sound in a live venue can change dramatically from sound check with no bodies in the room compared to a room filled with people for the actual show. If you have other bands performing before you, they can mess shit up with your gear and sound board."

"We know that. You usually have us only play five songs at rehearsal for labels," Rob said. "If we play a show at the Whisky, we should play more like a thirty-minute set?"

I jumped in. "Always keep it short and sweet and leave them wanting more. No more than fifteen to eighteen minutes. And you have to engage and connect with the audience. I don't care if it's one A&R person or fifty thousand screaming fans in an arena. You've got to be likable, charismatic, and able to talk even in the most uncomfortable situation, like if equipment is malfunctioning, joke about it, and be able to talk through the time it takes to fix the issue. But we are urging you not to do a Whisky show right now."

"What if the labels want to speak to us after?"

"They'll always ask the same questions," Danny said. "Who are your influences? Who do you see yourself touring with? How do you guys write? How long have you been playing together?"

"Have intelligent answers and always have an anecdote or fun story attached to each topic. Either way, a big showcase is too risky."

"This should be our decision. It's our band, our risk," Brad responded.

"Well, if you really think you're ready and can pack a room, then we won't stand in your way," I said. "And it appears by the irritated looks on your faces, we're outvoted six to two, so fuck it. We'll put all our focus on getting music executives out to see you at the Whisky. Just don't make us regret it."

On December 1, I took Brad to a beer garden in Westwood for his twenty-first birthday. The waitress brought our mugs of craft brew.

"Happy birthday, buddy. Here's to many prosperous years together. I am making you the promise that within one year from right now I will get you a major-label deal, Geffen or otherwise. I always keep my promises, even to myself."

"Thanks," he said, clinking our mugs, "but you can't make that kind of promise."

"I'm putting it into the universe. This time next year, we are signed to a major and on our way to stardom."

Brad laughed and took a sip. He winced at the taste and said it would be his last beer

"I love you like a brother, so, in all seriousness, we have a potential offer from Geffen coming and I just think that this Whisky showcase is an unnecessary risk. Please don't do it."

Brad looked me and in a calm voice said, "We want to do the showcase. You need to trust us just as much as you want us to trust you."

CHAPTER 12

WHISKY A NO GO

THE DAY ARRIVED. THURSDAY, DECEMBER 10, 1998. THE BAND was pumped for the Whisky show. My hands were jittery as I inhaled my Honey Nut Cheerios.

"Wish me luck," I said as I kissed Carmen before running out the door to the office. It was a big day.

By eleven o'clock calls were coming in requesting to have names confirmed for the guest list. Rumors swirled that certain top-level executives were hopping flights to LA to see Xero.

At two Danny called. "Today's the big day," he said, laughing nervously. "These guys better pull it off or we're both fucked. By the way, David Simone is travelling today. It sounded like he wasn't happy about the band doing a showcase, but I said we had it booked before you met with him."

I swallowed the lump in my throat as I ran to the restroom, my stomach in knots.

At five I walked to the venue to listen to the sound check. Brad put his hand on my shoulder. "You look stressed. Don't worry, Jeff. We got this." His smile calmed my nerves. Then he walked over to the sound guy and slipped him $150 to make sure the sound was good.

This guy better make the Whisky sound like Madison Square Garden, I thought.

By eight, the guys were backstage getting ready as Danny and I paced the empty floor. I knew we shouldn't have done a major showcase the week before Christmas when execs were at holiday parties. No one would be flying in from New York to sign a band this late in the year. *The band will be disappointed, but maybe this is for the best.* I didn't feel they were ready to throw all their chips on the table. I took a deep breath and began to relax.

At 8:45, Danny Goodwin from Virgin, Matt Aberle from Reprise/Warner Bros., and Michelle Ozbourn from Arista walked in. Michelle bought me a drink and said she had a surprise for me. Other than a few scattered people, the venue was empty.

At 9:30, Michelle came up to me. "Oh my god, Jeff, come here!" Peeking outside, I witnessed the longest line of limos I had ever seen. *What the hell is going on? They couldn't possibly be here to see Xero, could they?* We stood next to the box office as executives filed in. Michelle grabbed my hand.

"Clive, meet Jeff Blue. He's the executive who has been developing Xero and is responsible for Macy Gray."

Holy shit. Clive Davis, CEO of Arista, responsible for the likes of Whitney Houston and Bruce Springsteen.

"Pleasure to meet you, sir," I managed to choke out.

I shook hands left and right as I was introduced to faces I had only seen in the music trades: Tommy Mottola, the head of Sony; Guy Oseary, Madonna's right-hand man; and Polly Anthony, who signed Macy Gray, all flew in from New York City and gave me hugs.

Danny Goodwin grabbed my shoulder. "Hey, buddy, you got the entire music business out here! I pulled all the Virgin Records bigwigs out of a huge Christmas dinner meeting, so Xero better be legit tonight because my ass is on the line."

More handshaking. The Columbia staff, execs from Epic, Capitol, Atlantic, DreamWorks, RCA, Columbia, Reprise/Warner, and dozens of managers and tastemakers entered, all introducing themselves and patting each other on the backs.

Danny told me to relax, and we quickly calculated that with at least thirty top executives and tastemakers at the show, worst case scenario, we'd have at least three, maybe four major-label offers sitting on our desks by morning, in addition to the Geffen offer. If anything, this incredible turnout would make the Geffen offer higher. By the following weekend we'd be driving matching red Ferraris. Maybe the showcase wasn't a bad idea after all.

By 9:45 the room was filled with expectations, like we were going to witness the next Nirvana. The venue was so packed we could barely move. Danny and I looked at each other with huge smiles. "We're rock stars, bro!" Danny said.

"Not so quick, pal. This can go either way," I said, checking my watch. "Fifteen minutes to stage time." We had told everyone to be a half hour early because in this business everyone shows up late, but tonight, everyone was right on time. Executives began to fidget. I overheard a few people saying, "Where is this band?" One voice said, "Who's this guy Jeff Blue? That name has to be fake."

It was finally ten. "Show time, buddy," I said to Danny with a forced confidence.

Danny leaned into my ear. "This is our make-or-break moment. Legends are made on nights like this."

The background music stopped, and the audience was electric with anticipation. Ten seconds went by and the background hard rock started up again, but no band. People looked confused and irritated.

At 10:10, Danny and I ran backstage to check on the band.

"What are you guys doing? People are packed out there like sardines, all waiting for you," I said.

"We are building anticipation. You shouldn't have told people to come early," Mark said.

"We didn't want them to miss anything, but you can't keep executives standing around waiting. The venue is filled nine-ty-nine percent with industry legends and one percent family and friends. You need to get out there," Danny added.

"We will be out in a few. We're getting pumped," Brad said.

"Pump it on stage, guys. Come on," I retorted as we left them..

Making our way through the sea of executives, Danny and I surveyed the waning crowd. Five more minutes, and we were sweating profusely. Several people left the venue. Then, all of a sudden, music from the house speakers cracked through the tension like a thunderstorm. Danny and I crowded up to the front like schoolgirls rushing to see the Backstreet Boys. The lights went on, and the intro music started. All eyes turned to the stage. Looking back through the crowd, Danny Goodwin gave me a thumbs-up.

Thirty seconds of intro music seemed like an eternity. "What the hell with this intro?! Damn, guys, get on stage already," I mumbled under my breath as I turned back to see Goodwin's smile turning into a frown.

Finally, the band walked on: Rob behind the drums looking good, Dave, Joe, then Brad tuning his guitar. Danny muttered, "Come on, guys, start the song." Just as we saw a couple execs turn to leave the venue, Joe Hahn hit the turntables and started spinning. Brad hit his signature guitar riff, and they were off, com-pletely extinguishing random chatter. And then they stopped.

Is this a sound check? The band started tuning their instruments again. *Oh my god,* I thought. Looking back at the crowd, who were clearly confused, I started to feel dizzy.

A handful of executives departed during the lull, and two minutes later the band started up again. It was the real set. The guys played their hearts out, but something was off. The first ten seconds were intoxicating. Danny and I stood up front starstruck, but the excitement was short-lived with the realization that Mark's vocals were out of key. I prayed that no one would notice. Danny looked at me and mouthed, "Fuck." People noticed. The songs felt longer, and the venue's electric energy dropped dramatically. The thirty-minute set dragged until the last song was played. Stage lights went down, and the house lights came up. Danny and I clapped feverishly, letting out chants of "woot woot!" but our shouts were met only by echoes.

Looking at each other, we simultaneously turned slowly around to a virtually empty room. A few of the band's closest friends and family were clapping slowly. Danny's law partner, Scott Harrington, was just shaking his head. Crickets.

Danny and I walked up to Scott and clung to him like a life raft. "Guys, that was painful," he said. "It was like listening to cats and dogs fighting. You guys really screwed the pooch on this one."

I gulped. My throat was as dry as a desert. "Was it really that bad?"

"You guys were standing right there at the front of the stage like you were seeing a naked woman for the first time. You didn't notice the mass exodus midway through the set?"

"Oy," Danny muttered.

"You both have to go underground for six months after this show. Seriously, don't show your faces."

Danny looked at me before reeling back in horror. "Man, are you okay?" he asked. "You look like you're gonna..."

My stomach churned with fear and disappointment as my brain and body flip-flopped between deciding whether to vomit or cry. Both urges fought for first release while my dreams of the big cushy A&R job lay crushed alongside the half-drunk cups of Budweiser strewn across the sticky floor.

I managed to hold back my emotions and put on a happy face as Danny and I walked backstage. High fives, hugs, and handshakes, all with fist bumps. "You guys did a good job in a difficult room. I know how hard it is to perform in front of all those executives with so much on the line," I said.

"Are you okay?" Brad asked. "You look sick."

"Damn Subway. Musta got a bad sub. But you guys really played your hearts out." Danny and I didn't want to bring their spirits down, so we quickly left and walked back to my Toyota, where Danny and I shook our heads and consoled each other on how we had just screwed our careers. I couldn't stand Ferraris anyway.

Driving home through the dimly lit streets of LA, I rolled down my window to get some fresh air. My truck slowed to a red light. A guy in a yellow Lamborghini pulled up alongside me. I could have sworn he yelled out over his loud engine, "Your band sucks and you're out of a job," as he sped off. Now I hated Lambos, too.

Within the next thirty-six hours, we received seven official passes. The nail in the coffin came when Geffen Records shared the news that Eddie and David were out of their contracts, which meant my potential gig and deal for the band were off the table, regardless of how they had performed.

I went into the men's room and threw water on my face. "Fuck. You gambled, against your better judgment. The band has no deal. You have no A&R job. Your company, the labels, the band, the band's family, and your family, all relied on you, and you failed them. You can either walk away from this failure and sweep it under the rug like most execs do, or pick up the pieces and become stronger. Mike and Brad are in sync and poised for greatness. It would be hard to sway my belief in either of them, but Scott is right. Something needs to be done."

I could hear my mom in my head saying, "You still have your law degree to fall back on." What a wonderful way to ring in the holidays. Merry Fuckin' Christmas.

CHAPTER 13

ONLY AS STRONG AS YOUR WEAKEST LINK

THE FOLLOWING WEDNESDAY, STEPHANIE BUZZED. "JEFF, you have Danny Goodwin on the line."

"Yo buddy, we got a deal?" I asked.

"The deal? The deal is I'm fucking fired. Fired because I told my president and CEO how amazing Xero is. I pulled them out of their fucking Christmas dinner because you and Danny Hayes promised me the singer was going to be better. That show was a fuckin' disaster. They think I've lost my ears and my ability to discover talent."

"I have no idea what to say. I'm so sorry, man. Seems like we're all fucked."

That night, Scott, Danny, and I went out for drinks. The Goodwin firing and the bad reception we had made us the laughingstock of the industry. We could either walk away from the mess or put in the hard work to get the band back on track. We decided on the latter, but in order to breathe life back into this band, it meant replacing one or more members and rebranding them.

The next morning, Brad showed up at the office in good spirits and asked if I'd received any offers. Somehow, the agonizing look of despair on my face didn't convey the magnitude of the loss we had suffered.

"Is it bad?"

I motioned for him to sit down. "Brad, I'm going to be honest. It's worse than bad. It's cataclysmic. We need to call a band meeting."

"You said we did great. Are you joking?"

"No one wants to be the bearer of bad news when everyone is telling you how great you are. They always kill the messenger. But here's the fact." I swallowed hard. "Every single label passed."

"Really?" He looked up at me after a minute and smiled. "Well, at least we have Geffen."

"Brad, *every label*. Simone and Eddie Rosenblatt aren't even at Geffen anymore."

"What about Danny Goodwin? He loves us."

"You can visit him at unemployment. He's axed," I said, slicing my finger along my neck. "He stuck his neck out for you guys, and he was fired. Please call the rest of the band here and I'll go over the rest, but please don't bring Mark."

I knew what had to be done. Danny and Scott were convinced that Mark had to go, but I was the one closest to the band. I'd been in Mark's shoes before and the thought of going through his pain sent a shiver down my spine.

The following day, the staff was getting ready for the annual Zomba Christmas party that evening, hanging ornaments, caterers and bartenders setting up. It was a party that would be attended by hundreds of industry execs. The guys in Xero, however, looked like they were on a death march as they walked in, finally sitting in my office. They could feel the somber tone of the meeting before it even got started.

Danny Hayes and I sat on one side of my office with the band on the other.

"We know what you're going to say, so let's get to it," Mike said.

"Look, you guys are great, and Mark is a great guy, but plain and simple, you're only as strong as your weakest link. As you requested, we were able to get every top A&R guy and CEO out to see the band, and almost all the negative feedback was focused on the vocals. We need to rebrand this band and that means getting a new front man."

"This Mark situation was in the back of all of our heads. It's just not how we thought it would turn out. Is there something we can do other than to fire him?" Brad asked.

"No, guys. Jeff and I have a responsibility, not only to Zomba, but to you and your families. We like Mark, but we've got to make an executive decision here."

Digesting the information, Mike said, "From now on we want to know every detail from the showcases, positive or negative. Don't sugarcoat it. We don't care if it hurts our egos. If we don't know the truth, we will never grow as a team."

"Okay. From here on out, you'll know all details, positive and negative. Changing the name will help, but in order to get a record deal, we need to find a new vocalist who has the right chemistry with the band, right age, an incredible voice, presence, and star power." Standing up, I spun a quarter that was sitting on my desk. "Just realize this. If we do happen to find this mystery singer, it will put a focus on any other weaknesses. The band doesn't have to be perfect, but for a team to truly be strong it has to be a chain, with pressure spread evenly across the length, each link support-ing the next."

"In every city across the country there's someone willing to work ten times as hard as you," Danny added. "You guys are lucky that we all live in LA and Jeff gave you a publishing deal. We are here to help, but rest assured, someone else would kill to take your spot."

The band shook their heads and looked disgusted with me.

"Mark will be here for the Christmas party and I don't want to ruin it for him," I said. "But after the party, this Band-Aid is being ripped off."

CHAPTER 14

GARDENS OF GLENDON

THE ENTIRE BAND RETURNED THAT EVENING AND ENJOYED the party as if the meeting had never happened. Danny, Brad, and I approached Mark. "Hey, let's all go out next Wednesday," Danny suggested. "Let's do that place in Westwood, Gardens of Glendon."

"That's expensive. What's the occasion? Another Christmas dinner?" Mark smiled.

We had all agreed to tell Mark the bad news over dinner. Danny would ask, "What should we do to move forward?" At which point the band would gently bring up the idea that there needed to be a change.

We entered the beautiful restaurant situated near UCLA and sat down at a large, round table in the back. Twenty minutes passed without anyone initiating the conversation.

"So, how does everyone feel?" I asked.

"Good," the band muttered.

"Danny? How are you feeling?"

"I had a good day," Danny replied. "Merry Christmas, guys."

Shaking my head in disbelief and irritation, I stated, "Well, things aren't so merry this holiday. We didn't get any offers, and people weren't blown away by the show." Danny nodded and a couple of the guys moved uncomfortably in their seats.

"How did everyone feel about their performance? Mark, did you do your best?"

"Yeah, of course, I did my best. I mean, we could always do better, but we just have to keep working. You know, it's a process."

"Guys, what do you think?" I asked, looking around the table, waiting for the others to speak. The silence was deafening. "No comments? Well, I'm going to be blunt here. The main complaint was," I paused, "the vocals."

"The sound wasn't very good, and it was hard to hear through the monitors," Mark replied, nodding.

"Unfortunately, I don't think that's really the issue. With all due respect, I think your vocals need to be stronger," I said.

"I agree," Mark continued. "I'm going to work harder. I am going to get better. I mean, I think we all can get better. We just need to practice more."

"Mark, it's not an issue of practice. I just think…" I looked around the table, but no one chimed in to help me as I alone sat in this slowly sinking boat. "Well, we all discussed it, and I honestly think it's best if we look at other singers."

Mark looked like a truck had run over him.

Danny helped out. "Mark, this isn't about you directly. It's about what's best for the band."

"I'm glad this discussion is happening," Mark replied. "I'm going to work my ass off. Things are going to get better."

"It's too late for that," Danny said. "This has been going on for a while. We really feel we should look for another singer."

"This isn't your band. We started this band. Not you guys. I don't hear the band saying they want me out!"

Finally, the band chimed in. "Yeah, we all discussed it."

"Jeff, how the hell are you going to kick me out of my own band?" Mark stood up and stormed out of the restaurant.

Following him outside, resenting the fact that I was the only messenger of doom, I explained, "We're in a horrible situation because of the Whisky performance. What would *you* do if your singer was the primary reason every label passed? At some point you'd come to the conclusion that a change needed to be made. The band loves you, but we all agree this is necessary for us all to survive. I can only imagine your frustration."

"You can't imagine. You're not the one being cut."

"I was cut from a couple of bands, and I know it sucks hard. That's why I'm behind the scenes. We tried everything, and I just don't know what else to do."

"I kind of know you're right," he said, his head sinking low. "It's just hard to hear it. It doesn't look like things are going anywhere with the band anyways. I was thinking of leaving, to be honest."

"Listen, man, when one door closes, another opens. You're a smart guy and a strong leader. People listen to you. You still wrote some amazing songs. I still have to get these guys a deal, and I will do everything possible to make sure some of these awesome songs that you co-wrote remain on the album. But if this change doesn't happen right now, there won't be any band or any songs on any albums. Please trust me."

Mark's talents did shine through. He became a music manager, helping guide the careers of some massive artists and his song contributions appeared on *Hybrid Theory*. He never forgave me for that decision, but it was the decision that allowed the band to become Linkin Park. And it was just the first of many times that I would be the unforgiven bearer of bad news.

CHAPTER 15

IT'S YOUR BIRTHDAY

EARCHING FOR A NEW SINGER WAS A FULL-TIME JOB AND one filled with constant rejection. Simultaneously, Dave decided to rejoin his previous band, Tasty Snax. Kyle Christener took Dave's place on bass as the band auditioned replacement singers.

In late February I received a contract to renew my employment for another two years, until March 2001, along with a promise that I could leave at any time if I received an A&R offer. Richard and Neil were incredible bosses so I was thankful, after all the drama, to have a job, although I was doubtful they knew how much I appreciated them. Richard and I agreed to toast to the new contract at the South by Southwest music conference in Austin.

A month later, on Thursday, March 18, 1999, I stepped off an American Airlines flight in Austin, Texas. The most coveted hotel for label execs was the Four Seasons. My taxi passed the swanky spot as I dreamed of someday staying there. We drove on over the river to the opposite side, and I checked into the Embassy Suites where the indie artists and crew bunked. I threw on my SXSW badge and headed out to see the onslaught of hopeful bands playing their hearts out in the March heat.

It was around four in the afternoon, and all the high-level music moguls were drinking their expense accounts away at the Four Seasons bar. Danny's friend, David Christensen, had just secured a huge deal for his new artist, John Oszajca, and had sprung for an incredible suite with his newfound riches. I was sitting with David and Scott Harrington, who were reminiscing about how awful the Whisky showcase was. "Another round, Grey Goose sodas?" I politely asked the waitress trying to drown out the cloud of doom that still hung over me from that show. "On him," I added, pointing to David.

Scott raised his finger, slightly intoxicated. "Speaking of Grey. I wasn't going to say anything, but I may know this kid in Phoenix who can solve your problem. He just left his band Grey Daze. He's got a killer voice, but I don't know if the Xero guys would vibe him. They'd have to deal with having a real front man. This kid could steal the show and take the spotlight away from Mike."

"Having a two-front-man band has always been the goal. Mike is a team player. Who's this mystery singer? Let's call Mister Grey Daze up now!"

"I know he's working on a new project. Maybe you can sign him on his own. And why are you getting so excited? You've never even heard this kid."

"My first priority is Xero, so if he's that good, I don't want to wait. Let's call him now."

"Nah, man. When we get back to LA."

Our waitress walked up with our drinks. A tattoo of a musical note peered out from behind her ear, hidden by her short hair. "Gentlemen, your Goose and sodas. And just a heads-up, happy hour ends in ten minutes."

Looking at her name tag, I asked, "Amber, can you settle something for us, please? It's a simple yes-or-no question. Should my friend Scott here make a phone call or not?"

"Not sure who you're thinking of calling, but I vote yes, make the call. Sometimes you just gotta say, 'What the fuck, make your move.' And your friend here clearly wants you to," she said, winking at me.

"Did you just quote Risky Business? That alone is worth a thirty percent tip! Put it on his tab," I said, pointing to David again, smiling.

Scribbling her number down on the napkin and sliding it under my hand, she whispered in my ear, "Make the call."

"All right, I'll think about it," Scott said, draining his glass. "You're married, give me that napkin. I think David has a bottle in his room. Let's roll upstairs."

We went up to David's room, where a bottle of Ketel One sat atop of the TV. Pouring drinks for everyone, I toasted, "Here's to David. Congrats on the new signing, and to Scott, who is going to get this kid from Arizona on the phone right now."

"No way. Not now."

I picked up the hotel phone receiver. "David's even going to pay for the call," I laughed.

Scott reluctantly grabbed the phone and dialed. The phone rang three times, and he was about to put the receiver down when a woman answered.

"Hello?" Party music blasted through the phone.

"Samantha, it's Scott Harrington. I have someone from a publishing company who wants to talk to your husband. His name is Jeff Blue. He has a band that's looking for a front man. I recommended Chester."

More party music, and then a man's voice emanated from the receiver. "Hey, Scott, what's up? We're just in the middle of a pre-birthday bash."

"Hey, buddy, happy birthday. Sorry to interrupt, but my friend, Jeff, can be a little pushy. He's a music publisher from LA. You want to speak to him? He's standing next to me."

Scott rolled his eyes as he tossed the receiver into my greedy little hands.

"Hello? This is Jeff."

"Hey, Jeff, this is Chester!"

"Chester, hey man, I have a band in LA that's going to be huge, and we're looking for a singer. It's like a cross between Depeche Mode and Stone Temple Pilots, with hip hop. We also have a great rapper."

"Sounds cool. I love STP," he said. "Sorry, I can barely hear you. We just got back from Mexico." By now he was screaming over what sounded like Metallica in the background. "We're just having a little party."

"Well, happy birthday. Here's my gift." Scott rolled his eyes and shook his head as I continued. "I'm going to have my assistant in Los Angeles send you a demo tape with the band's songs, and then a tape without vocals. I want you to record your interpretation of what you think you could do to make the songs into hits. Completely use your own vibe and sound to show me something different. Give me personality and edge, something that makes me go, 'Fuck yeah.' Inspired and urgent. You feel me?"

"Yeah, I'm down, but it's my twenty-third birthday party this weekend."

"Look, I appreciate that, so take this opportunity of a lifetime and start your new year off right. I'll send you the tapes today, and I want to hear what your version of them by Monday when I'm back in the office. Cool?"

"Wait, you want me to miss my party? What the fuck?"

"What the fuck gives you freedom. Freedom brings opportunity. Opportunity makes your future."

"Isn't that line from a movie?" Chester laughed.

"It's a Risky Business quote. If you can't say it, you can't do it," I added as Scott pretended to stick his finger down his throat.

I could hear someone in the background say, "I'm booking the studio now."

"Sorry, Jeff, that's my wife."

"Look, man, follow her lead. As Wayne Gretzky said, 'You miss one hundred percent of the shots you don't take,' but you gotta do what you feel in your gut."

"I got it."

"Have a great birthday, Chester!"

I hung up the phone and glanced at Scott. "I kind of feel like a douche. Was I too hard on the kid on his birthday?"

"Bro, you are a douche. He's not going to leave his party to record a demo for you, especially after your non-inspiring diatribe. No more talking about Xero. And please God, no more eighties movie quotes. Let's grab barbecue. I'm starving. Jeff's buying."

CHAPTER 16

GAME CHANGER

SUNDAY MORNING I TOOK AN EARLY FLIGHT BACK TO LA. I couldn't stop thinking about Chester, who'd probably hung up the phone thinking, What a dick. I threw my bags on the floor next to the door and my body on the living room sofa. I needed to relax after a three-hour flight and a one hundred and twenty hour hangover, when my cell rang, blasting my neurons with an annoying melody.

"Hey, Mister Blue. How are you?" a pleasant, happy voice on the other end said. Last thing I wanted to hear was a salesperson.

"No telemarketers. Argggh!" I yelled into the receiver. "Do you want me calling you at home on a Sunday?!"

I hung up the phone. A minute later it rang again. *Unbelievable,* I thought. This guy doesn't quit.

"Listen, I don't want to buy a water filter, carpet cleaning, or..."

"I'm not a salesperson!" the voice screamed back. "I just wanna come out to LA?"

"I don't care where...Wait. Who's this?"

71

"It's Chester, from Arizona. I'm calling you about Xero."

"Chester! Hold on there, man," I laughed, sitting up as I held my throbbing head. "Oh shit. I'm sorry, I didn't know this number. And no one calls me Mister Blue unless they're selling something. Did you finish recording the tracks?"

"Yeah, I finished it all."

Pausing in amazement, I said, "You've got to be kidding. You left your birthday party? I thought I scared you off with all those movie quotes."

"Man, you inspired me, and my wife would have killed me if we didn't do it, so...it's all done. You want to hear it over the phone?"

"Right now? Okay, sure."

Chester put the phone up to his speakers, and the playback started. "Yo!" I screamed. "I can barely hear your voice; it's too distorted over the phone." Straining to hear his voice, I suddenly got chills. His tone cut through the distortion. I pressed the receiver to my left ear and plugged my right ear with my finger. My lips parted, and I mouthed "fuck" to myself as a surge of adrenaline shot through my body and my headache seemed to dissipate.

"What'd you think?"

"Wow, Chester, I could barely hear it, but what I *could* hear sounded really good. I can't believe you left your party. I really appreciate that. I'm impressed." I was shaking my head in amazement.

"So I'm good for the band?"

"That's a band decision. Send me the demo. But I promise you, if it's not with Xero, with your drive and attitude, you'll be a success. Thanks again for your intensity and diligence."

As I was getting up to leave the office the following Tuesday evening, my co-worker, Jon Firstenberg, tossed a manila envelope on my desk. "This ended up in my mail. I was about to toss it in the trash. It's from a Chester Bennington?" he said.

Damn, I thought to myself. *The kid did it.* I ripped open the package, ran to my car, and popped in the cassette. The first note of Chester's voice sent a shiver through my body, and a huge grin spread across my face. My eyes opened, and my heart leapt. The voice was hard, energetic, inspired, angst-filled, and urgent. I listened to the second track, which was even better. Arriving at home, I left my car idling in the driveway, blasting Chester's voice, unable to stop listening, and, after thirty minutes, my ears were ringing. I screamed, "Fuck! Woot, woot!" Leaping out of the truck, I danced in the courtyard with my two dogs, kissed my wife, and ran inside to call Brad.

"Brad, I found him! This kid is a game changer!"

"Found who? What are you talking about?"

"The new singer! For Xero! This demo this guy Chester sent me is amazing. You gotta hear it. Killer voice, driven, has his own sound, and looks like a star. You want me to play it over the phone?"

"No, man. I can wait till tomorrow," he said. "You met him? You have a picture?"

"Brad, he's a full rock star, tatted, ripped," I said, realizing I had no idea what he looked like.

"How old is he?"

"Old enough, just prepare for greatness."

"Jeff, all right, sounds cool. We'll see."

Racing into the office the next morning, I sat quietly at my desk and tempered my excited heart, tapping my fingers nervously on my desk, before I dialed Chester's number, careful not to sound too eager. "Hey, Chester, this demo is pretty solid. Looks like we just got a placement in this TV show *The Crow* for a scene with the character Draven."

"Cool, man, that's amazing! I'd love to come there and meet the band. They liked the demo I sent?"

"They love it. Just get here ASAP. I promise it will be worth it."

CHAPTER 17

BLIND DATE

That Wednesday afternoon when Brad came into the office to listen to the demo, I said, "First, I have some great news. 'Rhinestone' was officially licensed for the TV show The Crow."

"Cool. Maybe Mark's vocals weren't as bad as you thought."

"Sit down and listen," I said confidently as I blasted Chester's interpretations of the songs. "I'm telling you, this kid is dangerous and raw, with a magic in his voice that I haven't heard in a long time."

"He sounds like Scott Weiland. Not sure that's the vibe we're going for." Brad said. "I'm down to meet him, but you've got to get Mike on board before you do anything."

"This kid's coming in tomorrow morning. We're not going to lose any more time—or this kid Chester to another band."

Wednesday morning arrived, and I had on a black V-neck tee, blue jeans, and Vans, trying to look hip and cool. I said to my assistant, Ariana, "Let's clean up the office. Move that chair over near the window and straighten up this area, please. Move the stack of CDs off the drum set."

"What does this guy look like?"

"Honestly, I'm not sure, but I think he's buff, blond hair pulled back in a ponytail, tatted up, six-foot-something, with combat boots," I said, creating a picture of him in my mind based on his voice.

"You've never seen this guy?"

"No. I have no idea what he looks like. I was so pumped on his voice I forgot to ask for a picture."

"Oh my god. So this is like a blind date," she laughed.

"Don't say that." I replied, shaking my head.

"Well, it's a blind *musical* date. Does Carmen know you're cheating on her?"

"You need to stop. But that's funny. I've got butterflies like crazy! I have a feeling this is going to be special."

"You're such a dork," Ariana said.

Chester arrived and rode the elevator to the third floor. Stephanie buzzed my office. "Jeff, your singer is here." It seemed to take forever for Ariana to walk this mysterious singer down the short hallway to my office. When he finally arrived at my door, my mouth dropped in astonishment.

"Hi, Jeff. I'm Chester Bennington."

I was speechless. Picture a nerdy kid with glasses, frail body, and pocket protector. That was Chester to a *t*, minus the pocket protector. This was miles from the rock star I'd imagined and had described to the band. All I saw was a huge smile, bright eyes, and a glow of innocence that made me think he should be on the back of a milk carton. We needed someone visually intimidating behind those powerful-sounding vocals. But here was Chester with spiky, dyed-black hair, wearing a black glittery shirt that looked like it was bedazzled by some crazed fifth graders and was two sizes too big.

I politely left Chester in my office and closed the door. Ariana was holding back laughter, and I was trying not to scream.

"How's your date going? Not what you expected?"

"Not funny." I went into the conference room and called Scott Harrington.

"Scott. What the fuck?!"

"You like him?"

"This guy looks like he should be the president of the high school chemistry club. I promised the band a rock star. They're going to kill me."

"It's a good thing he looks geeky. It's alternative rock."

"I'm so fucked." I hung up the phone and popped my head into my office. Chester was looking at the plaques on my wall with a big smile on his face. Closing the door gently, I jumped into the neighboring office to see what kind of swag was lying around. A black Tupac promo tee, size L, was in a box. I stole the shirt and threw it into Chester's lap.

"Try this on," I told him.

"You don't like my shirt?"

"That sparkly button-down shirt doesn't really fit your voice. You should look like you don't care."

"Hey, what the fuck, man," Chester exclaimed as I tousled his hair.

"Just getting the spiky shit out of your hair. Image is very important, especially for a lead singer. These guys are understated. You gotta look like your voice. Let's do some jumping jacks, get that blood pumping."

Chester laughed, and any nervousness or self-esteem issues seemed to dissipate. I spent the next thirty minutes getting to know him. He seemed sweet and innocent. But behind the innocence, I sensed a dark side. Instead of looking at him as a voice, I saw a vulnerable, tender spirit. That demo he sent me had to be a therapeutic release for all that angst and gut-wrenching emotion pent up inside him, ready to explode. I just needed to find where it was hiding.

"Jeff, the band is here," Stephanie informed me over the intercom.

"Okay, Chester. The guys are going to love you," I said as his eyes twinkled under the fluorescent lights. The band entered and everyone stood, looking at each other without uttering a word. Chester looked like a deer in headlights as he awkwardly put up his hand to wave.

"Hey, Chester. Nice to meet you," Brad extended his hand, followed by Mike and the rest of the guys. "We like the demo you sent. Great voice."

There was an awkward silence I was eager to break. I put my hands on Chester's shoulders. "Why don't you all hang out and then you guys can roll to the rehearsal room." I knew in my heart that Chester was our guy.

Following that meeting, four weeks passed during which the band continued to audition singers as well as rehearse with Chester. At the beginning of the fifth week I got a call from Chester. "I appreciate everything you've done, but I need to talk to you in person. Can we meet up and grab a bite?" he asked.

Chester walked down Sunset Boulevard, past the nice restaurants, and pulled up a metal chair at a pizza spot down from the Whisky a Go Go.

"Chester, you look like shit. Are you okay?"

Looking defeated and ignoring his pizza, he replied, "I can't thank you enough for believing in me. I love the band. They're all incredible, but I'm not sure I'm what they're looking for. I'm not trying to be a pain, but I need to know if I'm in or not, or else I have to get home. The band keeps auditioning other singers while I've been sleeping on couches at my wife's parents and cousin's houses or sleeping in this green piece of shit Toyota Tercel. I know what you were able to do with Macy. Maybe you can sign me to a development deal?"

"First, eat. Take a deep breath. The guys just take a while to make decisions. It took them nine months to do my publishing deal. I know you can't wait that long, but I do know they want you."

"I'm couch surfing, my wife is back in Phoenix, and..."

Interrupting, I said, "I know you're stressed. But to be honest, the guys are just doing their due diligence. You're the best singer I've heard in a long, long time, but it's got to be their decision. I know they love you."

Chester looked defeated, and his shoulders slumped.

"I didn't realize you were sleeping in your car," I said. "Give me a few days. I'm heading over to see everyone later this evening." I hugged Chester, and a tear welled up in my eye. There was no way this kid wouldn't be a star. I'd bet my life on it. "If you need a place to crash tonight, you're welcome at my house."

He sighed heavily, "I'm good tonight. By the way, you may get a call from my wife."

"Okay, should I be scared?" My sentimental tear froze halfway down my cheek.

"No, she's awesome. She just wants to talk to you."

An hour later Stephanie buzzed me to say, "Chester's wife on two."

"Hey, Sam."

"I appreciate everything you're doing, Jeff, but I don't want my husband to be strung along. I don't want to seem like his manager, but he needs to be happy and find the right project. We've both put our lives on the line because we believe in you. If this isn't the right band for him, you will help us find his future, right?"

"I completely understand your position. I have your back."

Feeling pressure from all sides, I headed out to watch the band audition another singer. After he left, I closed the rehearsal room door.

"Guys, what's going on here? Is Chester in or out?" I asked, emotionless yet nervous on the inside.

Mike held his hands up. "We've thought about this a long time." My jaw was clenched so tight I could hear the enamel on my teeth peeling off. "We saw a lot of great singers, and Chester, well Chester wasn't good..."

"Jesus, are you kidding?" I blurted out.

"Chill. Chester isn't that good. He's great. He's our new singer." Mike laughed, and a wave of relief passed over us all. "We'll let him know tonight."

"Wait? He's in the band?" I sighed with relief. "This is awesome news. Congrats!"

CHAPTER 18

HYBRID THEORY

Samantha and Chester came over that weekend to celebrate his new gig as the lead singer of Xero. Handing me two six-packs of Corona, they entered the house and we cracked some bottles open.

"Do you know how stressful these last six weeks have been?" Chester asked.

"Yes, I do. I was right here with you, man," I laughed.

"We are going to do great things, Jeff."

"This is just the beginning. You've made it out to LA. Now the hard work starts. I can't wait for you to get in the studio and hear what you guys come up with. You and Mike are going to be amazing together."

"I'm so excited. We decided to start rehearsing on Monday and begin writing new songs. But, for now, let's drink."

We raised our bottles and toasted the future.

The following week, I walked out of the bright sun shining on Hollywood Boulevard into the dark rehearsal studio, my eyes struggling to adjust to the dim lighting. I gave Chester a big hug as he wrapped the microphone cord around his elbow and wrist. I could tell he was a little nervous.

"Chester, you aren't nervous, are you?"

"No. Well, maybe a little. This is the first time you're seeing me in action since we've started writing new songs."

"Dude, you're amazing. Just be yourself." I put my arm around his shoulder. He jumped up and down a dozen times as if to shake off his nerves, like a boxer in the ring getting ready for a fight. My adrenaline spiked.

The guys started tuning their instruments. Brad looked down at his pedals, his earphones on top of that mop of curly hair. Rob had a nervous smile on his face as Mike, always confident, paced the floor, clearly ready to go. Joe sat behind his rig and started scratching. To my eyes, the band was finally looking like a *band*. As I sat on a stool watching him move, Chester came up to me, singing his heart out, his warm breath hitting my face. He was too close for comfort, but I had nowhere to move. He owned the moment. He owned the imaginary stage he was on. Right then, I was in *his* world.

After a few minutes of my eardrums being blasted, and blinded by my excitement for the band's completion, reality set in.

"Guys, I see the chemistry. I feel the energy and presence, but there's still something missing."

"Is it me?" Chester interjected. "Am I not putting enough energy into it?"

"Not at all. You're intense as hell. In fact, I still have your spit on my face. All of you are amazing. I'm just not sure I hear a hit yet. Generally, in order for a band to get a major-label deal, they need a fan base, some press, or maybe some local radio. We don't have that, so everything is a headwind for us. What Xero does have are great writers and performers. In order to break out above the rest of the cred bands in the market, use your strengths.

You need hits. And after the Whisky showcase, the name Xero has a stink on it.

Mike nodded. "We were actually discussing that very concept. Now that we have Chester, we felt the need to reinvent ourselves. We came up with some ideas, and I think we are set on the name Hybrid Theory. It kind of represents our sound, blending rock and hip hop. Mixed media, you know?"

I expelled a huge sigh of relief. "Wow, I love it. New singer, new name. I can't wait to hear the new Hybrid Theory songs."

"Brad and I are coming up with a lot of ideas," Mike said. "We'll come by your office next week with some tracks. We're super excited about this!"

CHAPTER 19

ROCK, PAPER, SCISSORS

I MET ROB BOURDON AT HIS APARTMENT IN SANTA MONICA. AS I stepped over dozens of jiffy padded envelopes strewn across his carpet, he said, "I'm mailing all these demos out to our street team. We are really working hard at building it as much as possible."

"That's awesome. You're really being proactive," I said as we grabbed our surf boards and loaded them into my 4Runner.

We made it to the ocean and jumped straight in. The waves were chill that day, so to pass the time we sat on our boards playing rock, paper, scissors. Rob's relaxed demeanor made him one of the nicest guys in the band and the only original member other than Brad, and now Chester, that I hung out with socially.

"How do you feel the band is coming along?" I asked him.

"Honestly, I know I need to get tighter. I'm in the rehearsal room nonstop. Mike's beats are complex. I just want to make sure I get everything right."

"Dude, you are committed, and it shows. You have a huge heart. You'll get tighter. What about Chester?"

"I think he's coming along well. It's hard, you know? We've all known each other for a long time. He's a little different, but he's gonna be good."

"Cool. I know you are all still finding your chemistry. This will happen. You have my word."

"What makes you so sure?"

"I don't know, Rob. It's so weird. Just the fact that you and I are sitting in the ocean on a Friday afternoon when I should be at the office, and we are talking about music. It just feels right, doesn't it?"

Just then a fin was darting right at us.

"Holy shit."

"Oh my god. It's not stopping."

We were both paralyzed with fear. The fin dove deep under us.

"Dude. I thought that was a shark!" Rob exclaimed.

"We're still alive! There's no blood or body parts floating in the ocean!" I said. "It must have been a dolphin. But dolphins don't come straight at you, do they?"

"That must be a sign!" Rob said. "You're right. We're gonna get a deal."

"No. That's a sign that we should get out of the fuckin' water right now!" My heart was still racing with fear. "You will get a deal though, Rob. I promise."

I returned to my office just as Chester was arriving unexpectedly. "Hey, I'm headed to rehearsal with the band, but I wanted to stop by. I have an idea," he said.

"What's up?"

"I'm thinking of changing my name."

"Your name?"

"Yeah. I was thinking something cool like Chaz."

"That sounds like you should be wearing a pastel polo shirt with the collar turned up, some khaki shorts, and penny loafers. You just gotta be you, man. Be your sound, your own identity. Be the fuck-you version of Chester Bennington, the guy who screams his ass off in key and doesn't give a fuck when he spits on them while he sings. That guy is Chester."

"Well, I'm gonna try out Chaz for a while, but I'll probably keep Chester."

"More importantly, how are the songs going...Chaz?" I said, laughing.

"We're working on them. I think the guys want to come over and play you what we've got."

CHAPTER 20

CARRY ON WAYWARD SON

It was early May. Mike and Brad rolled into the office. A CD came flying into my lap, and the two young musicians laughed heartily.

"Let us know what you think about these new tracks."

I looked at the white CD scribbled with black sharpie, arrows pointing in different directions, and Mike's pager number inside. The track listing read:

Over to Me (Blue)
Could've Been
Rhinestone
Esaul
Part of Me
Turn to Grey
Pictureboard
Ashes (unfinished)

Mike moved over to the drum set and sat down while Brad grabbed the electric guitar that was sitting in a stand directly in front of my desk.

"You want me to listen to this now?" I asked. "In front of you?"

"You wanted to hear what we came up with, so yeah," Mike said as he reached over to my stereo and pressed play.

"Make yourselves at home," I said sarcastically. "You know, I do have a full-time job that requires me to do other work," I said, knowing that my comment went in one ear and out the other.

"We know you can't wait to hear it, so don't pretend otherwise," Brad said, smiling.

Brad was right. I couldn't wait. My anticipation was so strong my heart raced as I placed the disc on the tray.

The song "Blue" began with a filtered muddy guitar, followed by a hooky bass line and then Mike coming in with an incredible rap. I was immediately intrigued. Then Chester's voice came in with a weak pre-chorus, followed by an equally underwhelming chorus. I cringed. I felt an inexplicable anxiety creep in. I could see Mike and Brad analyzing my facial reactions as I scribbled notes on a yellow legal pad.

It wasn't as strong as I had been hoping. The second chorus ended, followed by a Nirvana-style breakdown accompanied by a beat. My ears perked. I always appreciated Mike and Brad's ability to come up with compelling parts. Although I liked this part, the deviation didn't seem to fit. Just as I was getting frustrated, Chester's vocal came in with a soaring melodic bridge that seemed like it was sent from heaven. My heart leapt and my eyes opened. I got chills. *This* was special. *This* was identifiable. *This* was inspiring. The guys could see it in my face.

"So, what do you think?"

"I notice it's titled 'Blue,'" I laughed.

"That's just a temporary name," Brad said. "Don't get a big head. What did you think about it?"

"I have goosebumps on my arm. The bass line is sick, and the guitar riff is killer, and, Mike, your verses are amazing."

"Is it a hit, though?" Mike asked.

"It's like half a song. It needs a new chorus. But, holy shit, that bridge is phenomenal."

"That's not exactly what we wanted to hear, but at least we have something to work with. Keep listening."

"Could've Been" started with Chester singing in a beautifully tortured voice accompanied by a pretty acoustic guitar and simple bass part, followed by a solid electric guitar riff. Mike blasted in with his rap while Chester accented background parts. Chester's chorus again failed to have a good hook. The song felt forced and trite. I was overcome with worry. I had pushed for Chester, and he seemed to be the weakest link in these two songs. This was not the magic I had hoped for, and the guys could see it on my face. At the end of the song, a random bass line, à la Flea of the Red Hot Chili Peppers, raced in at breakneck speed, and although it didn't fit whatsoever, I was intrigued.

"You didn't like it?"

"Seems like you're having a hard time finding the right blend."

"Check out track four, 'Esaul.' You've heard us play this live."

"Yeah, I always love this. Classic Brad with the killer guitar line. This song has potential, but Chester's vocal could be stronger."

"Part of Me" had another classic guitar line from Brad. "The arpeggiated moody scary stuff seems like your calling card. Kind of like a horror movie soundtrack."

"So you like it?"

"Parts of it are decent. Let me listen to 'Turn to Grey,'" I replied, pressing play. "I like this initial guitar line. Cool rap and guitar interplay. I do love Chester's sweet and light singing, and this delayed vocal stuff at the end is cool, but the song as a whole? I can't remember anything in this song to sing back. Let's hope this song 'Pictureboard' is better. Didn't you mention this song before?"

"Yeah. We are really proud of this one. We wrote this way back with Mark, but Chester's singing on it. It's one of my favorites."

"Seems like you guys are trying to write a hit. And it doesn't feel right. I like Mike's bridge. I notice you like to use the 'rainfall' lines. It's a common theme in most of your lyrics. At this point I'm looking to narrow down our list of songs to record for an album. I'm not feeling this one at all."

"This is one of the songs we definitely want on the album. It's hooky and easy to sing back."

I rubbed the knots developing in the back of my neck. The tension in the room was growing. I definitely heard the band growing musically, but the songs weren't hits.

"I don't mean to be negative," I said. "I just want to make sure we don't settle. Let me hear this next song, 'Ashes.'" I hit play. "Oh, hell yeah! I love the personality that comes out in this. It sounds like you're having fun. When Brad says, 'Mike perfect tempo, give me any number and I can rap to it, ready? One hundred! Go!'— that makes me feel like I'm sharing a special moment with you guys. I love the Spanish guitar, and, Mike, your lyrics are really cool. You're telling a story, which is nice. I like Chester's cinematic lyrics and how they interplay with the Spanish guitar."

"So you like this one?" Brad asked hopefully.

"Ehh, no," I said shrugging my shoulders. "The song as a whole is kind of underwhelming. That song 'Blue' with Chester's bridge has promise. It's insanely good."

"We may do that song 'Slip' that we did with Mark. You love that song. We may put Chester on that."

"Ah, yes, I like 'Slip.' There's some good stuff in that song. And you have more of your dark rain references," I laughed. "Your lyrics always make me connect with muted colors, like gray. It's interesting and a good quality that a writer has a color associated with him."

"What are we missing?"

"I hate to be the music exec with the 'I don't hear a single' line, but I'm gonna be that guy. I like songs where you hook the listener right from the top, make an impact, then get out. I'm a huge fan of call-and-answer hooks, which you and Chester could do so well. These songs meander. I want to hear songs that have intense, dynamic peaks and valleys, but ultimately run straight for the touchdown."

"You go by the 'Backstreet Boys of rock' handbook of writing," Brad joked.

"Whatever," I responded.

"No, that's a compliment. Backstreet Boys have great songs. They're well-crafted hits. I understand what you're saying."

The guys left, and I sat back and listened again. There was something here, but it didn't have the chemistry I had hoped for.

A week later I decided to send the new songs to Michael Tedesco and Scott Harrington, since he was the one who had referred Chester to me. My phone rang the following day.

"Jeff, what the hell? I'm driving down PCH cranking these demos. What happened to Chester's voice? Where's his trademark growl? It sounds like prog-rock Kansas."

"Kansas? I don't think it's that bad. And don't ever dis 'Carry On Wayward Son.' But I agree there's something missing."

"It's disappointing. You and I both know Chester can do better than this," Scott replied.

"I agree. Macy Gray and her new artist are coming down to Hybrid Theory's rehearsal tonight. After she leaves, the band is showcasing for a few labels."

Later that evening, Macy walked into the rehearsal room on Sunset across from the legendary Jumbo's Clown Room. "Hey, Brad. I haven't seen you since Jeff's wedding. He keeps telling me how amazing you guys are."

"Congrats on your deal!" Brad replied.

Macy gave the guys a hug and introduced us to her new artist, who grabbed the mic and began to sing a cappella. After a couple minutes, Brad jumped on stage and broke out an early-'80s R&B riff. Rob and Joe threw a beat down, and the female singer tore into amazing vocal runs, following the band's groove.

What happened next left an indelible impression on my memory. Chester grabbed a mic and jumped on stage next to Macy's singer. His voice soared as he created a beautiful melody, harmonizing with Macy's singer before transitioning into his signature growl, erasing any doubt in my mind about him being a one-of-a-kind talent. Macy leaned over and whispered, "This band's got something, and your new singer is the real deal."

When Macy left, the record labels, along with Danny Hayes, all filed in, to see Hybrid Theory. The band lit up the cold rehearsal room as Danny and I stood and watched in awe. The new chemistry was undeniable, but all three labels left saying, "I don't think it's for us. The new singer's got a great voice, but it's just another rap rock band."

Chester looked crushed. I took him aside, put my arms around his shoulders and gave him a hug. "Man, you have no idea how great you just performed. Your ability to blend your beautiful, soulful, R&B voice and transition into the heavy shit is what will separate you from all the other singers in the universe. If these A&R idiots can't see what's right in front of their faces, then fuck 'em."

That next morning Michael Tedesco, the head of A&R for Jive Records, called me. "Jeff, I got the demos you sent. Spend some money and get someone to produce new demos with the new singer. There are a lot of great producers around; you just have to find the right one."

"That's already in the works. Mudrock, who produced the Godsmack album, agreed to produce some new songs. We start in two days."

CHAPTER 21

HORSE

THE BAND WAS IN THE STUDIO WITH MUDROCK FOR ABOUT a week. Meanwhile, Epic launched Macy's single "Do Something" on June 29, 1999, and for all the hype she received, the song was considered a flop. During this time, Hybrid Theory performed more showcases for Reprise, Atlantic, Radioactive, Capitol, Columbia, Mercury, American, Virgin, Jive, RCA, Arista, and several others. Everybody passed. All my hopes and dreams seemed to be melting away in the June heat.

Chester knew I was depressed and decided to stop by my house on a Sunday with a six-pack and a big smile to cheer me up.

"We're just hitting a bump in the road." Grabbing the basketball from the driveway, Chester said, "Let's play Horse. You drink every time you miss and answer a question."

"Man, I suck. I'll be wasted." Bouncing the ball on the pavement, I threw the first shot, which bounced on the rim before falling in. "That means you take a drink," I said to Chester. "My question is, are you happily married?"

"I love Sam. I think I want to have a baby with her as soon as we get a record deal. What about you and Carmen?"

"I love her. She's just been on me like crazy about how much time I spend on my career. But we're okay." Looking at each other, we said at the same time, "I'll drink to that!"

Chester eyed the net and sent the ball flying. It bounced off the backboard. He grabbed a fresh beer. "I bricked. You get to ask another question."

"Who do you get along with the best in the band?"

He paused to consider his answer. "I honestly don't know."

Just then Samantha and Carmen walked out. Samantha had heard the question and added, "Chester gets along best with Rob. He's so easy and a breath of fresh air."

"I feel you," I said. "I love surfing with Rob. I have a lot of great times with Brad, too."

Samantha grabbed the ball and a beer. "There's a power thing going on with the band," she said.

Chester cut her off, "Look, it's all good, I just want us all to feel like a band. A second family."

"Jeff will have your back, honey," Samantha said as she and Carmen walked back into the house.

Changing the subject, he sipped from the bottle. "What do you think about the roughs I gave you?"

"I'm not loving it so far. The songs have got to be universal, something that everyone can relate to. Touch my deepest fear. I don't know if I feel that in any of these songs."

"That's not what I wanted to hear," Chester replied. "But, I have plenty of fucked-up shit in my head to write about. Shit that happened to me when I was younger."

"Man, I'm so sorry. Shit, Chester, you can always talk to me."

HORSE

Throwing the ball at the backboard and completely missing the hoop, he said, "You need to tell the band your thoughts on these songs."

"I have a ton of opinions, but I'll leave that job to whoever ends up A&Ring your album."

"I got you, man. Maybe it will be you," he said smiling. He tossed the basketball in the air with one hand, the other hand holding the beer bottle, and *swoosh*. The ball effortlessly entered the net. "See man, that's a sign. You're going to A&R our album."

"From your mouth to heaven's ears, bro. Let's just get you a deal."

CHAPTER 22

CBGB

It was late July, and I had the new Mudrock demos in hand as I arrived in Manhattan. The plan was to head to Rome, New York, for Woodstock '99 and hang with Korn and Limp Bizkit before returning to the city for meetings with the Jive executives. It was clear, no matter where I went, people knew I was about to pitch Hybrid Theory.

Watching the incredible concert from directly on stage I imagined Hybrid playing with bands like Rage Against the Machine, Red Hot Chili Peppers, Korn, Limp Bizkit, and Metallica. It was late as I climbed onto the bus of a band I knew and took a seat toward the front. The bass player approached and offered me a bump of coke.

"I'm good," I told him.

He turned to his lead singer and said, "Jeff does a bump or he's off. I want to bring that blonde chick waiting outside, and Blue's taking the only available seat."

"Give him a break," he said.

He motioned to the blonde outside the window. "Babe, I got you a seat. I want to do lines off your chest. Blue, you're off."

"You're not kicking Jeff off," the lead singer said.

"Then he's sitting on the floor." The bassist led the girl up the stairs and into my seat. I didn't care. I just wanted to get back to the hotel. That was something I respected about Hybrid—their no-drug policy.

The lead singer apologized profusely. "Sorry, bro. At least you got a ride."

My heart was heavy. I felt like this moment was a culmination of all the rejections of the past year, another slap in the face reminding me how neither I nor Hybrid Theory fit in.

After the three-day concert, I went to check out bands at CBGBs in the East Village. The smell of cigarettes was imbedded inches deep into the stucco walls plastered with fliers and graffiti. I sat on a barstool, sipping my Heineken, when I noticed a tall gray-haired gentleman to my right.

"Hey, you like this band?"

"Not really my thing. There's not much substance. Kinda faceless."

"That's how most everything is these days," he laughed. "Hi, I'm Joe McEwen."

"Oh, nice to meet you. Jeff Blue," I said, shaking his hand.

"You're at Zomba, right? I remember getting a tape from you on Macy Gray. I'm head of A&R at Warner Bros."

After a brief conversation, he invited me to come to his office.

Having been rejected by Warner three times prior, I was hesitant to breathe a word about Hybrid Theory. I was let into Joe's office by his assistant and sat across from his desk. Neither of us spoke at first, until he leaned back in his chair. "So, what are you working on? Developing anything new?"

I reached into my Tumi bag, almost laughing, thinking, *Here comes Warner Bros. rejection number four*. I felt like a used car salesman. "This is what the band calls 'mixed media.'"

"Hybrid Theory," he said as he read the cover and nodded his head, listening quietly to all eight songs without interruption. He seemed bored shitless as he stared out his window over the cityscape.

He left the CD in the tray, shifting his gaze to my direction, and I braced for the inevitable. "It's different. I like the lyrics, the arrangements are intelligent, and the transitions through the songs seem to tell a story. The band sounds like they have more vision than the other bands out there."

I sat up in my chair. Did he say he liked the band? I was like a fisherman with his pole in the water and no bites for so long that I was in shock when I finally got a tug on my line. "Joe, these guys are a different breed." *Don't oversell him*, I thought. *Slow your pitch.* "They're cerebral, thoughtful, conceptual. I appreciate the fact that you see and hear that."

"Out of everyone you know, who do you think would be a good A&R person for Warner Bros.?"

"There's some great people out there. Tom DeSavia from ASCAP, Evan Lamberg at EMI publishing..."

Joe sat back again. "What about Jeff Blue? Why didn't you mention yourself?"

"Oh," I laughed, astonished. "You should speak to him."

"We should keep in contact. I have a good feeling about this," Joe said, smiling.

I left Joe's office ecstatic but not wanting to get my hopes up. I had been let down by too many people too many times, but this felt too good to ignore. I walked back to the Zomba corporate apartment, through the park, feeling a renewed energy. As soon as I opened the door, I dialed Brad's number.

"Warner Bros. may be interested in hiring me."

"That's great news. You'd bring us along?"

"Do you seriously have to ask?" I laughed. "Come on. Wherever I go, you go. I won't leave you hanging."

The following day I entered the New York Zomba offices, took my seat in the boardroom with the other executives, and played Mudrock's songs for Clive Calder, the CEO of Jive and Zomba. Clive placed his hands together and looked at Michael Tedesco.

"Any thoughts, Michael? Last we spoke, you said the biggest concern was that the band had no street credibility like Korn or the Deftones."

"Korn and Deftones are kicking at the radio doors, but Hybrid Theory could be the band to break through if they have real hit radio songs."

"Maybe we can put together a development deal," Clive suggested. "Jeff, let's keep an eye on the band and see what they come up with in the interim. There's no rush."

Things seemed to be changing with interest from Warner Bros. and Jive. I could almost taste the sweet promise of what was to come. I hopped on a flight back to Los Angeles the next day and called every A&R exec, every label, and every manager I knew to come check out a special Hybrid Theory rehearsal showcase. I even convinced Matt Aberle and David Kahne to give it another go.

The band performed for David and others like they were in front of fifty thousand screaming fans. Chester's powerhouse voice blasted within inches of David's face. It was so close, so intrusive, yet so confident and powerful, that I felt exhilarated and uncomfortable at the same time. I'd never seen a better showcase in my career. I was certain the labels would be blown away.

I had just witnessed a stellar performance, but every label in attendance passed again! We were supposed to be past the rejection phase. I walked back to the rehearsal room disappointed, but I put on a huge smile.

"You guys were fuckin' great. I gotta run to a meeting though. Keep up the good work!"

Before they could ask any questions, I walked to my 4Runner and screamed at the top of my lungs, "What the fuck am I missing?" I wasn't sure if I was sad, lonely, or just exhausted from being told we weren't good enough.

CHAPTER 23

HERE'S SPIT IN YOUR EYE

Gary Kurfirst walked into the rehearsal room with a bottle of water, tapping it nervously with his fingers. "Sorry, it was a busy day. But you got me back down here, despite that Whisky showcase," he laughed.

"Trust me, this new lead singer is a game changer. Think about all those bands that were rejected and came back and proved to the world that they were wrong."

"You're saying these guys are going to change the world? You're setting the bar extremely high. Don't get me wrong, I want you to have a win. I brought out the troops for you," he said, motioning to the five executives with him. "You've got radio, product manager, and A&R. I'm in your corner, but I'm not gonna sign a band because you were a good intern eight years ago. I like you, but not that much," he laughed.

I walked into the hallway where the band was getting ready.

"So who's this guy?" Joe Hahn asked.

"He and the crew out there are from Radioactive/MCA. The guy is awesome. He signed the band Live—you know, 'Lightning Crashes.' He also worked with Shirley Manson from Garbage, the B-52s and the Ramones. He's a visionary who sees things early. Plus, I think we've been rejected by every label, so he's pretty much the last one standing. I was an intern at MCA back in 1991 when I met him, so rock his world."

"We got this. We're gonna slaughter him," Chester said, patting me on the back.

I walked back out and took a seat next to Gary. The band came out, Joe Hahn started the beat, and the band exploded with what I thought was a flawless performance. Brad's execution was intense, Rob seemed to lock in with Joe, and Mike came out swinging like a seasoned fighter. Any doubt I had was extinguished when Chester straddled up to Gary and sang full blast into his face. I could feel his hot breath through my nostrils from three feet away. A vein protruded from Chester's temple. I felt a drop of water, then another. Chester's sweat swung out of his pores as if there was a slight drizzle from above.

Gary had nowhere to move. He was captive to Chester roaring like a tiger. When I thought it couldn't get any more elevated, three minute droplets of spit emanated from Chester's mouth and landed in Gary's eye, forehead, and upper lip respectively. I repressed a nervous laugh. Chester didn't seem to notice, until Gary put up his hand and Chester moved back on stage, oblivious to the body fluids left behind.

My laugh swelled in my chest so much that it ended up in tears. Gary wiped his face. Chester was a beast, and I could only hope that Gary was impressed and not as concerned about the face shower Chester just gifted him.

Mike moved around with a confidence fueled by anger, and the band left nothing out. It was rage, clear intensity, and focus. If I were an A&R guy, I'd stop the entire audition and sign them on the spot. Shit doesn't get more real than the performance I was witnessing.

After the show, the band was drenched in sweat. The MCA executives stood up and glanced at their watches. They shook my hand. "That was incredible," the radio promo exec said.

I was proud as hell of the band. I swelled with admiration for them as I looked to Gary for a comment. "That was one of a kind. Definitely different than the Whisky show. Walk me out to my car to discuss. We're just running late to a dinner meeting."

I looked back at the band, who seemed to be rightfully proud of the set they had just performed. "Be right back," I said, winking at Brad, who was smiling ear to ear.

I caught up with Gary. "Jeff, you know I respect you, but that was a bit much."

"What do you mean?" I asked, my excitement deflating quicker than a popped balloon.

"The band was okay. I don't hear a hit."

"They haven't been able to rehearse the new songs, but I think they're amazing."

"The new singer is good, but he was in my face so much that I couldn't really get a feeling for the band."

"I thought he was amazing. Just picture what he'd do in an arena. He's a star."

"Thanks, but I'm respectfully passing. Let's do lunch," he said, climbing into his car.

I walked back into the rehearsal room where the guys were breaking down their equipment.

Brad nodded. "I can tell when you think we did well. We all feel pretty good about it. What'd he think?"

My shoulders slumped, and Mike said, "Really?"

"Guys, I don't get it. That was by far the best showcase I've seen you do."

Rob's animated face turned into a frown. His drumsticks dropped to the floor. Brad laid his guitar in his case. "I don't know how much more we can do. I thought we played our hearts out."

"You did. That was fucking amazing."

"You're not a good judge. You like everything we do," Mike said. "What were their exact comments?"

"First, they didn't hear any hit songs. I totally disagree. I think you're writing better songs, and I know you aren't ready to perform them, but I do know you'll come up with better. More importantly, your performance was insane."

"We all felt really good about it. So, they didn't make any comments about the show?"

"He did make a comment about Chester," I said as Chester's face lit up.

"The one thing I can say, is that I know you gave the performance of a lifetime. I was blown away. But you gotta respect personal space. I mean, I could smell what you had for lunch. Smelled like bean burrito."

"That is what I had. Bean and cheese, 7-Eleven. I was in a rush. How'd you know?" he said.

"Because I could friggin' smell it when you were singing, and I was a few feet away." I laughed.

"Fuck. I just lose myself in the performance. I can't help it. It's like a bomb explodes inside of me."

"I get it. Just don't let it explode out onto someone else. Come on, guys. You need to be able to laugh at the situation. You can't be upset. You did great."

Mike shook his head. "Of course we can get upset. This is our future. So, that was it? We were too close for comfort?"

"They were in a rush to go to a company dinner. I'm sorry. I'll take you out to dinner. Something better than Subway."

"No, thanks, I'm exhausted," Mike said. "I appreciate it, but I think we're gonna take a break tonight. Maybe we can all meet up tomorrow evening and discuss it further. Let's all meet after rehearsal."

"Sounds good," I said as Chester nodded to me.

"I'm down for dinner," he said, smiling. "I can get used to sushi."

CHAPTER 24

THE NEW CHEERLEADER

Two days later, I entered the rehearsal room on Hollywood Boulevard as the band was arguing about something related to the DJ mix and Joe's rig moving around while the guys jumped up and down. There was tension in the air.

"Hey guys, how's it going?" I said, knowing I shouldn't have asked.

"I think we're all getting a bit frustrated. Feels like the harder we work, no matter what we do, some label finds a reason that we're not good enough. It's exhausting, and now we're all getting stressed."

"Guys, no one said this was going to be easy. It takes time and hard work. I know you're working hard, but bands can spend five to ten years touring in piece-of-shit vans around the country just to get to this position. Just give it a bit more time. Last night was awesome and should be encouraging, not demoralizing."

"I'm running out of time," Brad said. "My parents are really pushing for law school."

"Mine are getting impatient, too," Mike said.

"I've been locking myself in this room nonstop practicing every day for hours at a time. Like entire weekends," Rob said.

"Guys, I know you're all working your asses off. That's part of the journey. Someone will see it and freak out just like I did."

"We've auditioned about forty times all over again for every major and indie label that exists. Radioactive was the last one. There's no one left."

Chester stepped forward. "Come on. I've never heard you guys like this. I know you've been working longer on this band than I have, but I think we're fucking awesome. We're just finally getting our momentum together."

"Chester, it's not the same, man. We are in a different place. You've got a wife and..."

"And what? We left Arizona, moved here. I've been sleeping in cars, couch surfing, and moved my entire life around for this. I'm totally dedicated, and we are gonna get a fuckin' deal. Right, Jeff?"

"Yes. You are. I know this is totally frustrating. I'm here too, guys. And Chester's right. You're beginning to have amazing chemistry. There's no way I will allow Brad to go to law school," I laughed.

Brad shook his head. "This is serious. We can't just do this forever without a deal."

"Give me two more months. I will get you a major deal. I promise this to you and to myself."

"You said the same thing on my birthday," Brad said.

"Yes, I've still got four months left on the birthday promise I made to you so you can hold me to that."

"Who would hire Brad as an attorney anyways?" Chester joked. "Let's get back on a positive vibe. You're family to me, and there's no way we're gonna let one another down. I'm more pumped than ever to prove everyone wrong. We're gonna have a number one album, and all these A&R posers will be like, 'Ah fuck, I should have signed that band.' Fuck those guys. We are gonna be the biggest band in the world, and no one is gonna stand in our way."

I scratched my nose at the heartfelt-yet-corny speech. It was from Chester's soul, and I appreciated the sentiment.

"Give me the four months left on my promise. If I don't come through, do what you need to do."

"Jeff, we're not giving up. We're just frustrated. Come here, Chester," Mike said, putting his arm around Chester's shoulder.

My heart warmed as if I was watching a movie where the underdog team of misfits talks themselves up for the big game. But in this scenario, there were no more games on the schedule. Regardless, I was inspired and happy to see them in better spirits, especially being led by Chester.

CHAPTER 25

THE GOLD CLUB

The first week of August, I was in Atlanta bonding with A&R exec Brad Kaplan and the Warner radio team. After a heavy steak meal, they insisted we go to the Gold Club. The stretch limo brought us to a massive building with gold lettering.

"A strip club? Guys, you know I'm married."

"You're not married when you're a thousand miles away."

After passing through the huge doors and the even larger bouncer, the building opened up into a bevy of neon lights and loud music. I stared not at the women doing seemingly impossible acrobatics on chrome poles but at the top NBA and NFL players scattered around the place.

Brad offered me a drink and said, "We want you at Warner Bros. Joe really likes you. Plus, we like your band, Hybrid Theory."

"That means a lot to me. I'd love to bring Hybrid to Warner."

We left it there and spent the rest of the night having a blast. The confidence I gathered at the Gold Club, however, was short-lived. Once I was back in LA, I got a call from Brad Kaplan.

"Just want to give you a heads-up. Joe and the president of Warner are meeting with Clyde Lieberman today at the Ivy for lunch. They're looking at him for your position."

"What? I thought he wanted me for the job." I was depressed.

A few hours later, Joe McEwen called requesting a lunch meeting with the president, Andy Shoun, at the Warner Bros. commissary. The writing was on the wall. Clyde gets to eat at the celebrity-packed Ivy restaurant, and I get taken to the office cafeteria.

A few days later, I was picking at my overcooked burger in agony as I spoke to Andy about my vision and my dedication to Hybrid Theory. I knew that at any minute I was going to hear that my friend, Clyde, was being offered the position, so I took one last sip of my fountain soda and braced for the inevitable.

"So, when can you start?"

"Start?"

"We want you to come to Warner's."

Knowing I was back in the game, and sensing some leverage, I quickly refocused and replied, "I'd love to be at Warner. I think we can do amazing things, but I want to make sure I can bring along my band, Hybrid Theory."

"Bring along?" Andy asked.

"Yes. Me signing as VP A&R, and the band signing simultaneously as an artist to the label. It would be my first signing." I smiled nervously.

My stomach clenched as we looked at each other. Andy replied, "We appreciate your dedication to the band. But we usually don't make signing a band part of an employment deal. It's two separate contracts. Is that non-negotiable?"

"Honestly, it's a sticking point. I'm even willing to make my contract and bonus contingent on their success. Whatever it takes."

"If that's the case, we should set up a showcase for Joe at SIR in Hollywood. I like your confidence and dedication; it shows you're passionate."

This would be our forty-fourth showcase, and it was the most important one, so I called Mike and gave him the news.

CHAPTER 26

S.I.R.

MONDAY, AUGUST 9, 1999, WAS A BEAUTIFUL SOUTHERN California day with temperatures in the seventies. The band and I walked through the back entrance of the famed SIR Studios on Sunset Boulevard at 1:00 to set up and sound check for the 3:00 p.m. showcase.

"Guys, these next couple hours will determine everyone's fate here in this room. You've got the best showcase room in California, you're the best you've ever been, and you're performing for the best record label in the country. Nothing can go wrong. Our lives depend on it," I laughed.

"Way to take off the pressure," Rob said jokingly.

"Where's the sound guy?" Joe asked, as the band began setting up.

The sound tech walked in five minutes later and threw a wrinkled bag with a half-eaten In-N-Out burger on the console. I smelled the semi-cold fries in the bag. He gestured to me and asked, "You want some?"

"No, I'm good, man. Thanks, but this is a *really* important showcase," I said, without trying to sound too annoyed. "I just want to get this moving and keep the band warm."

"Gotcha. It will sound great."

"Thanks, man. I know SIR is the best there is." I patted him on the back as the band began to soundcheck. The tech moved some knobs, followed by a lot of cracking sounds, then some popping noises. He shook his head and said, "Let's try swapping out these XLR cables." Mike began pacing the stage. I put my hands on my head, trying to remain calm as the tech pulled on his goatee and took a deep breath, looking at the sound board, and then at me, like I might have the answer.

"I'm not sure what the problem is," he said. "This rarely happens."

My mouth dropped open. "You gotta be friggin' kidding me. Please get a supervisor in here. We have a major-label showcase in thirty-five minutes. And please throw out those stale fries. The smell is driving me crazy."

The tech disappeared for ten minutes. I was about to blow my own fuse when another tech, who also smelled like In-N-Out, walked in and began fussing around the board. After fifteen minutes the band was up and started rehearsing. The sound was better, but there was still something wrong.

"Hey, man. I appreciate that you're trying to fix this, and this studio is awesome, but you know this doesn't sound right."

"I totally agree. We have to get someone to check out the board. I'd move you guys into another room, but there isn't one available."

Throwing my head back in disbelief, I said, "Please, please, do your best. We don't have time. I've got the head of A&R at Warner Bros. walking in that door any minute. I can't have—"

Before I could finish my sentence, Joe walked in the room with Clyde Lieberman and Brad Kaplan. *Why is he with my competition?*

"Joe. Hey, buddy," I said, exhaling as I introduced him to everyone in the band, all of whom were visibly stressed due to the soundboard issue. "We are having a little issue with the sound. I hate to make an excuse, but..."

"That's fine, guys," Joe interrupted. "I can hear through the sound."

The band got on stage, moved around nervously at first, and proceeded to start the set. The sound wasn't as horrible as I anticipated, and I looked over at Joe McEwen, who was actually smiling. He seemed to like the way Chester was able to deliver his angst and passion. Brad had his signature earphones on, Rob kicked ass behind the kit, Joe was killing it on the turntables, Kyle was in the zone, and Mike possessed the stage with confidence.

Chester came up to Joe's face screaming, sweat dripping down his face, and Joe smiled again. Despite the venue, the pressure, and unorthodox scene, the guys gave a great performance. Joe stayed for fifteen minutes after the show and asked questions that demonstrated a legitimate interest. He wasn't checking his cell phone every twenty seconds like many often do in this situation.

I walked Joe out to the parking lot, and we shook hands.

"I loved it," he said.

"They were good," Clyde chimed in. "I guess we'll catch up in a bit." They left together and I was left to wonder what would happen next. I was especially impressed with Clyde's integrity. Almost anyone else would have dissed the band in the interest of self-preservation, but he seemed honest and sincere.

Tuesday and Wednesday crept by, and finally Thursday morning at nine I received a call from Joe. "So, I've been tossing the idea around, and I think you can bring a lot to Warner Bros. Let's get our A&R deal signed, and then we can discuss signing the band once you're in-house. I know that's important to you. Great guys, by the way."

"Joe, I appreciate that, but I gave them my word, and it's got to be part of my deal. I'm going to see the band in Tempe, Arizona, on the twenty-seventh at the Big Fish Pub. There's other label interest," I said, lying through my teeth. "Not sure what I can do at this point. By the way, the band is writing new songs."

CHAPTER 27

WE NEED HITS

DANNY HAYES CALLED THE NEXT MORNING. "WARNER REALLY wants you over there. Congrats."

"I want to go to Warner, but we can't let it happen without me signing Hybrid," I said.

"I got you. Let me get out a proposal to Rick Streicker at Warner legal. He's working on your contract. I'm putting it together now. First paragraph reads, 'Between Xero and Warner Bros. Records. As we have discussed, the following proposal is subject to Jeff Blue's signing an employment agreement with Warner Bros.' That's pretty clear. They can't sign you without signing the band as a condition of your employment."

"You said the band's name is Xero."

"Well that's still the band's official name. I can change that later. What if you change the name again? Knowing you, that's bound to happen," he laughed. "How are the new songs coming along?"

"We still need a single."

My office rang. "Hey, that's Chester now. Let me hit you back."

"I'm calling you from a payphone, dude. We've got a few new songs. All the stuff you were telling me about how my vocals didn't really flow with Mike's. I think we may have something. I know Mike wants to present it to you. Can we come over to your office?"

"Of course. Can't wait to hear this."

The following week, I met Mike, Brad, and Chester, who were sitting in the Zomba lobby's red pleather sofas with smiles on their faces.

"I hear you have something good for me."

The guys filed into the office. Brad grabbed the usual guitar off the stand. Mike sat at the keyboard and Chester got behind the drum set. "Are you guys gonna jam, or is this a listening session? And why do you look nervous, Chester?"

"I feel like my parts were what have been holding us back from having something that labels will think is a single."

"Dude, your voice is amazing. Just let me hear this new demo and see where you guys are. Relax."

I stuck the nine-song demo in the CD player. The first song was "Untitled." "Great name for a song," I said with a smirk. The song began with a simple hooky piano line. A smile rose on my face. I tried to remain poker-faced, but the smile kept creeping back. I got that highly oxygenated feeling, tingling in my nose, and was so happy that I felt a tear well up.

"Are you okay? You look like you're crying," Brad said, concerned.

"A bug flew in my eye earlier. I'm fine."

"So? What do you think?"

"Wow. Where do I begin? The song is exactly what I hoped for. You guys totally figured out how to blend your vocals. The hooks are incredible, the beat moves the song along well, nothing steps on anything, it's seamless, and the song is a perfect pop structure. On top of that, a hauntingly great, intelligent, lyrical hook. 'In the

End.'" I nodded, understanding the importance of the lyric. "'It doesn't even matter.' Fucking textbook great pop songwriting. I'm inspired. That piano line is quintessential. I love it."

"Points of Authority" was next. I hit play, and my shoulders relaxed. "Guys, this song has so much promise. I love the guitar stabs."

"Mike took my guitar into Pro Tools and cut it up."

"It's brilliant, musically, and I love Mike's rap. It feels like I'm living inside an action video game. It maneuvers and swerves like a race car. But something is missing. The chorus isn't satisfying to me, so please figure that out. And the bridge is kind of a letdown. Work on this one because it could be incredible."

After we listened to "Super Xero" again, which I liked a lot, the next song was "I Hate You/Crawling." The song began with Chester screaming, "I hate you so much right now." Chester and I locked eyes as I listened to him sing the haunting melody. The lyrics struck me, engaging my senses. Then the chorus hit like a bolt of lightning. It sounded like an undeniable smash. "This is the 'Blue' melody. Mike, you outdid yourself. Perfect songwriting. Even the bass line is perfect, and nothing overwhelms or steps on anything. Except..."

"Except what?" Mike asked.

"Your bridge is redundant. It takes me out of the moment. And again with the raindrop references in every song. Otherwise the song is a fucking hit. Chester. Wow. Your vocals are stupendous, and Brad is getting his own identifiable tone. I love the way you work the chugs and harmonics. Those are such calling cards. But most importantly, your lyrics are powerful and personal. I feel sad yet inspired. The songs make me feel like I'm watching a suspense movie like *Halloween*. Arpeggiated piano, minor chords with major accents, cool beats, very cinematic and moody, with some really hooky, heavy guitar. This is what differentiates you from other bands. Plus, you're really getting great at leaving plenty of dynamic space for the breakdown verses that give it that personal breath where you really focus on the vocal. This is exactly what you need. All I can say is wow. You did it. Now you just need a first obvious single."

"You just said you thought these songs are the best we've done."

"What you've done here is set the bar."

"Set the bar of what?"

"You guys now have done such an amazing job, that every song on this album should be this good or better. In my opinion, these are no-brainer, record deal, sign-on-the-dotted-line singles. However, we've seen the trajectory of the responses. Just do me a favor and write three new songs with the intention that that they need to be better than 'Untitled,' 'Points,' and 'Crawling.' If you can even get one song that's better than these, one that's an undeniable first single, then this is a home run. I'd bet everything in the world on it."

The guys just shook their heads.

CHAPTER 28

JUST LIKE ROCKY

The band reached a milestone. Mike, Brad, and Chester truly clicked now. They had a sound, and more importantly they had songs.

I sat in my chair with a stack of twenty CDs including "Crawling," "Untitled" (which would later be retitled "In the End"), and "Points of Authority." Before I could send these out, I had to ask myself if it was worth being rejected all over again, but felt there was no way anyone could say these weren't radio smashes. I FedExed twenty CDs to all the major labels. One more round of showcases. Bring it on! I was inspired.

The phone rang two days later. "These are good. Really good," Danny Hayes said.

"The band's really come up to the next level. It's like some Rocky Balboa–type shit. These guys have experienced more rejection and just keep coming back punching harder and harder. I admire the fact that they don't give up. I'm excited to hear what people think of these new songs."

The next day Chester came to the office for lunch. Just as we were about to leave, the phone rang. "Columbia," Ariana said.

"Well, you want to hear this?" I looked at Chester. "It's the head of A&R."

"Yeah, this is exciting. If you believe in it, I'm sure everyone else will too," Chester said confidently.

I hit the speaker button so Chester could listen in. "Thanks for sending these other songs. These are better, but I didn't get it before, and I don't get it now. You know Reprise just signed Disturbed from Chicago. That's identifiable. Jonathan Davis is identifiable. Fred Durst is identifiable."

I cringed as I looked at Chester, who looked saddened. "This vocal duo: Mike and Chester. This is the double the power. The lead singer is a total star with a better voice than anyone out there. The hooky call and answer style with the rapper. And they have hits. Did you actually listen to the CD?"

"Of course. I guess I just want to hear something special."

"Well, thanks for listening," I said as I hung up.

"We have what it takes, Jeff. I won't let you down," Chester said.

"You've never let me down. These songs are hits. You're a superstar, Chester. The entire band killed it."

"I feel like we did too. I won't let that get me down. I know you'll find us a home."

Chester got up from his seat. "Subway sandwich?" The phone rang.

"Tedesco just called while you were on the phone with Columbia. He asked you to call him back," Ariana buzzed.

"You want to hear Tedesco's reaction?" I shrugged at Chester.

"Sure. Why not? I kinda like the rejection," he laughed.

"Allow the rejection to fuel you. So many people give up. But we're fighters. The ability to listen, evaluate, and retool strategy is what makes you a winner."

"You should be a basketball coach."

"I suck at basketball."

"True. You do suck. Just call Tedesco."

"Here we go," I said, dialing his number in New York.

"Jeff," Tedesco answered enthusiastically. "These songs are good. Much better than the EP. Chester and Mike found their chemistry. What's going on with the band?"

"Well, Chester's in my office right now."

"Hey, Chester. Good job on these songs. I wish I could get Jive to move faster."

"Thanks, Michael. That means a lot."

"I'd love to come see you guys again when I have a moment. But this is definitely an improvement. I'm taking you guys bowling."

"Bowling?" Chester questioned.

"There's an old-school place in Santa Monica. It's got a cool vibe. See you in a week!"

"Chester," I said hanging up the phone. "This is the beginning. This is your Rocky moment when you're training, punching the beef in the cooler."

"Wow, Jive must really love us. They're taking us bowling!"

"Are you being sarcastic?"

"No, I love bowling!" he answered.

"Well you're a cheap date, pal. Now let's get your Subway sandwich. I'm buying," I laughed. "After we finish eating, you can go and write three more hits."

CHAPTER 29

NOTHING IS FREE

I SAT IN MY OFFICE AND LISTENED AGAIN TO THE NEW SONGS Mike had delivered to me along with his written notes. Mike was clearly becoming a strong writer, but at the time I didn't know how much he was actually responsible for, as he created most everything in his room. I assumed the rest of the band wrote with him, and it was never discussed because our publishing deal was inclusive of all the members. Mike gave me a brief background along with the CD.

"Part of Me" was the song that, according to Mike, was the "obsession with one's own shortcomings and alleviating them." "Untitled (It Doesn't Matter)" was one of my favorites, although I felt the verses needed some work in terms of the lyrical phrasing. I then read the description, in which he wrote that during the process between the time he started the band and before signing with Zomba and me, when they were meeting various music business people, the band had been promised many things by shady people who prey on young bands, promising them the world and not delivering, and the band needs to remember that nothing is free in life. "Untitled" was about how it's important to create music for the people you love, are inspired by, and those who equally find inspiration from the band's music, because that's all that truly counts. I knew they met with people before signing with me, but I wondered who promised him things and didn't deliver. All I knew was that he was my responsibility, and I would make sure he had the best deal possible.

Then there was a song called "Flower" that I would later find on "She Couldn't," which, despite being an intelligent and beautiful song with nods to Depeche Mode, didn't feel like it was strong enough for the album.

Overall, we had three new songs that would make the album, and I was happier and more confident than ever before! I couldn't wait to hear what other labels thought about these songs when I went to New York a couple weeks later.

CHAPTER 30

BIG FISH, SMALL POND

IT WAS SEPTEMBER 16. I WAS IN NEW YORK FOR THE CMJ (College Music Journal) Festival in the middle of Tropical Storm Floyd where I met with Epic Records's Polly Anthony and Jon Polk and Island Def Jam label head Lyor Cohen.

The timing was good since early testing was indicating that Macy Gray's "I Try" was going to be a hit at radio. Suddenly, people were requesting A&R employment meetings with me. I played the new Hybrid Theory songs for every label I met with. Jive, Island Def Jam, Epic, and Warner said they were preparing written A&R job offers. I told Danny to accept whoever wanted to sign Hybrid Theory. Right now, that was only Warner. I decided to take a well-earned vacation with my wife.

While vacationing in Puerto Rico, I received a call from the CEO of Sony, Tommy Mottola, who said, "Let me make this brief. We want you at Epic Records."

"I'm about to sign with Warner."

"Whatever they're offering, we will double the salary."

I stood there in my hotel room with my mouth open, unable to speak.

"Jeff, are you there?" I was still stunned when I heard him say, "Fine, we'll add another hundred thousand. I understand you're in Puerto Rico. We are going to fly you to New York. I'll have a helicopter waiting, if need be, and have you sign tomorrow."

"Wow, I'm honored, but I already gave my word to Warner. What about my band, Hybrid Theory? Warner is allowing me to sign them as part of my deal."

"Let's bring you into Epic and then we can worry about the band after. I haven't seen them, but I am sure we can approve it."

I hung up the phone. Carmen and I ordered a bottle of champagne to celebrate. Overlooking the ocean, we toasted our second glass as the phone rang. My manager said, "I told you never to agree to anything. You already gave a verbal acceptance to Warner. You can't accept two offers."

"I don't have any written offers yet, and I've been banging my head against a wall for years trying to do A&R. I just want to make an album with my band. That's it."

"Well, you need to call Warner right now to cancel."

I called Warner CEO Russ Thyret's office immediately, as I gazed out over the beautiful coastline.

"We can't match Sony's offer, but we can meet you halfway," Russ said. "We'll sign Hybrid Theory and you as a dual deal with you as VP of A&R and executive producer of whatever you work on. We need someone who understands how to develop artists. By the way, I felt the same way about Prince as you do about Hybrid."

"You signed Prince? Next to Queen, he's my favorite artist. I think Hybrid has the potential to be iconic, too."

"Epic has too many rock bands, and Hybrid Theory could get lost there. You'd be a big fish in a small pond here at Warner. We can get the band's paperwork moving today if you agree. Just know that we will never pressure you—I'd never call you on vacation. As long as I'm here, and I don't plan on going anywhere," he laughed, "you will have full autonomy, and no matter what you decide, I will be a fan of yours."

"The salary isn't as important as being able to make an album with my band, with a label that believes in the project. If Hybrid Theory has a home at Warner, then so do I." I felt a huge weight lifted as I accepted the lower salary. For some reason I felt good taking less, as if there would be less pressure on me, less pressure on the band, that we could fly under the radar, and just make the best album possible, drama free.

Danny Hayes reached out to Michael Tedesco to tell him I was planning to leave Zomba to go to Warner Bros. Richard Blackstone called me minutes later.

"What is this I'm hearing about you talking to Warner Bros? We just signed your new contract. It's for two years."

"You made me a promise that if I ever got an A&R job offer, you'd let me go."

"I remember. Let me see what I can do."

CHAPTER 31

GOOD NEWS, BAD NEWS

I was at the Zomba office in New York when Danny Hayes called my cell.

"Do you have a place where we can talk?" he asked. "Alone?"

Stepping out into the hallway, I pressed the cell phone against my ear.

"So good news and bad news. Good news is I should be receiving short form deals for both you and the band from Warner Bros. Bad news is Zomba is still insisting you stay until March of 2000, which is another five months. In order to get you to Warner, though, Warner has graciously agreed to give Zomba points on the album. They really want you there."

"Thanks, Danny. I won't be back 'til next week. I would love to be there for that—re-create the publishing deal signing."

"I just sent all the documents to Brad to review. The band will be coming in tomorrow for a meeting about the details. What a wild ride."

"The ride is just beginning," I said. "We've still gotta make an album."

The band arrived in Danny's office at Manatt, Phelps, & Phillips through the same hallways, past the same yelling attorneys, past the commotion and into the conference room.

"So this is it," Brad said as he looked over the short form. "Nice Warner Bros. logo and everything."

The conference phone in the middle of the large table rang, and Danny pushed the red button. "Put him through," he said. "Guys, someone wants to talk to you."

"Hey, guys, I just wanted to say congratulations. I wish I could be there to celebrate," I said over the speakerphone.

"We're so excited. We'll celebrate when you get back," Chester replied.

"Did you get out of your deal?" Brad asked, concerned.

"Jeff will be out of his deal soon," Danny said. "Looks like he'll be official March of next year."

"I promise nothing will stop us from moving forward on finding producers and getting your songs tight. I'm taking you all out to dinner on Wednesday when I come back to celebrate."

"As long as it's not Gardens of Glendon!" Brad joked.

"What's wrong with Gardens of Glendon?" Chester asked.

"That's where Jeff fired Mark, our previous singer," Joe answered. "You go to Gardens of Glendon, you're gonna get whacked. Like the Godfather."

"Okay. Anywhere but Gardens of Glendon," Chester replied.

"We'll do the Rainbow, across from the office."

I smiled as I closed the phone and walked past the lobby with the massive Zomba logo. I was about to start another chapter in my life!

CHAPTER 32

F%*K LAW SCHOOL.
I WANNA BE A
ROCK STAR!

THAT FOLLOWING WEDNESDAY THE BAND MET IN MY OFFICE around eight in the evening and walked across the street to the famous Rainbow, under the awning and past the patio, the walls strewn with pictures of rock 'n' roll history and insane decadence. The smell of music history was embedded in the red booths. Platinum albums hung on the walls.

Chester said, "Dude, that's Lemmy from Motörhead over there. Holy shit. And that's Ron Jeremy in that booth."

"Yeah, you need to sanitize that booth before entering," Joe joked.

The waitress led us down to the long booth in the back. We scooted in, and the band studied the photos around them. "This place is great," Rob said.

"Someday you'll have some of your plaques in here," I said as the waitress brought our beverages. I raised my Diet Coke. "If you think about it, there's a few people and moments in your life that literally change the trajectory of your history. I first want to toast Brad. The kid who entered my office and never left. To Mike, with your relentless dedication and constant vision for writing and leading the band. Joe and Rob for bringing in the flavor and sound that otherwise wouldn't be Hybrid Theory. And here's to Chester. The guy I called, when we were both drunk, who left his birthday party to record a demo for a random music exec he spoke to for only two minutes on the phone. I mean that shit doesn't happen except in the movies. But this is real life. Someday we'll be telling our grandkids about this. Whether you make it huge or not, I applaud you. None of us in this room has let rejection, adversity, and the highest of roadblocks break the spirit of this band."

"And we've seen our share of roadblocks," Brad added.

"Here's to you guys and to a great future. Cheers!"

Everyone raised their glasses when Joe said, "Jeff, you never told us how you got in the business."

"That's another long story but very similar. I also met someone that changed my life forever."

"Now's the perfect time to tell it," Chester said.

Let me take you back about eight years to September 1991. I was walking up to the double doors of Geffen Records on Sunset Boulevard.

"Nice tie," a guy with hair flowing almost down to his ripped Levi's said, bumping into me as he jumped into a Ferrari with a parking ticket plastered on the windshield.

Holy shit! That was Axl Rose from Guns N' Roses. I entered the building thinking I looked cool in my khakis, a flowery tie, my long hair in a ponytail, and an angel dangling from my ear. Immediately

I felt out of place among musicians and executives dressed in ripped jeans and T-shirts walking past as I waited patiently in front of the receptionist who didn't seem to know I existed. All of a sudden, a smiling guy in his late twenties, brown hair, and flannel shirt walked in and greeted me with a bro-hug.

"What's with that tie?" he laughed, extending his hand. "I'm Craig, and you can ditch that day job soon, buddy."

Leading me around the corner to his office, I sat down on the lush sofa and could feel the history of the rock star asses that had sat in that very seat before me.

"My brother said amazing things about you," he told me. "You guys went to UCLA together, huh? That's cool."

"We were in the same fraternity," I said, hypnotized by the plaques covering the hallway walls, ranging from Guns N' Roses to Aerosmith to the Eagles to Whitesnake.

"Jeff, your drumming is awesome, and I know you do a lot of the writing in your band, which I totally respect. Look, I know you have a lot of opportunities to sign to all the majors, but Geffen is the most artist-friendly label around." He walked past me to open a massive metal filing cabinet. Stacked inside were hundreds of CDs that glowed like the Holy Grail. "Take anything. Whatever you want. It's yours," he said, handing me dozens of discs. "*Your* plaques will soon be up on this wall. *Your* CDs in this cabinet. I want to sign you to Geffen Records."

My breath caught in my chest. "What? That's fucking amazing," I exclaimed, as the stack of CDs dropped from my hands, scattering all over the floor. "Oh my God. I'm so sorry. I'm just so surprised and a little nervous. I'll pick this all up."

"Man, don't worry about it. I'll get someone in here to clean them up," he responded with authenticity and charm. "What about your singer? We should get him in here today right away."

"He gets out of USC law school at four. No problem!"

F%*K LAW SCHOOL. I WANNA BE A ROCK STAR!

Craig stood up and put his hands on his desk. He looked like he was about to propose to me with a tear building in his eye. I felt emotional myself, like my life, for once, was on the right track, unencumbered by parental and societal expectations, free to finally do what I wanted to. Fuck law school. I wanted to be a rock star.

For the next five minutes, he spoke about how fantastic I was, how my future was so bright, filling my twenty-two-year-old mind with dreams of private jets, recording sessions in top studios, international touring, and all the female attention it was sure to bring. Starry visions of signing my name in lipstick on a beautiful girl's chest danced through my head. Craig was my new favorite person in the entire world. Then he said, "I was blown away by your show at the Whisky last week."

"Um, you mean the Madame Wong's gig?"

"You did a secret showcase at Wong's? Fuck." He shook his head, hitting his hands on the desk. "What labels were there? We can beat any offer." He seemed to be getting anxious.

"We haven't played the Whisky. We've been trying to get a gig there for months. Can you get us in?"

The room fell silent. He squinted his eyes, and his mouth dropped open. I immediately felt the sofa get hard and uninviting. Shaking his head in puzzlement, he said, "What the fuck? I'm confused." After ten seconds of staring at me with his mouth open, he finally said, "Oh my god." He put his hand over his face in disbelief and disappointment as both our realizations aligned. I wasn't who he was expecting. I suddenly felt like an idiot—an idiot in a polo oxford and flowery tie.

"I can't believe this. I'm sorry, man."

"Wait," I said wavering between fury and despair, watching the most exciting moment of my life croak and bleed on the floor of this magical office. "Are we still doing a record deal?" The deafening silence was broken by the sound of crunching

CD cases under my feet as I stepped toward him. Reality hit me like a sledgehammer. There would be no planes, no studio, no lipstick-signed boobs.

"No! Sorry, man. There is no record deal. I totally thought you were someone else. This is just a total misunderstanding. You're a nice kid, but you gotta go, and please don't step on any more CDs."

At that moment, I made a decision that would change my life.

"I'm not leaving," I said. It wasn't bravado. I was unable to move. All I could do was talk. "What exactly do you do here, anyway?" I heard myself say.

"What?" he responded bewildered. "I do A&R. I listen to demos and go see bands. The ones I believe in, I try to sign to the label."

"You make money doing that?" I was busting my ass in law school and couldn't grasp the concept of a job where you get paid to listen to music.

Craig sat down on the edge of his desk, trying to calm his nerves. "Honestly, man, I thought you were in another band. I'm not trying to be a dick, but everyone's trying to sign them. If you really want to understand about A&R, I'm talking on a panel at UCLA tonight. Just buy a ticket to the class."

"Can I be your intern?"

"No," he said emphatically. "But you can pick up all those CDs and put them back in the cabinet."

A few hours after our meeting, I snuck into Craig's panel and sat in the last row. As I listened to him talk, I thought, I, too, wanted to develop and discover talent that can change the world. Law school suddenly felt like a small town I couldn't wait to escape. My pulse quickened, my vision seemed more vibrant, my thoughts had more meaning. I hadn't felt this inspired since I sat down at my first drum set at age thirteen. I knew exactly what I was going to do with my life. I was going to be an A&R person.

Brad was shaking his head in disbelief. "We owe UCLA a lot for the introductions it's brought us," he said.

"Yeah. It was six years later, and I was teaching the exact same class that I snuck into."

"So how did that transition into you meeting Brad?" Chester asked as he took another bite of pizza.

"After I left the UCLA lecture, I decided right then and there that A&R was my life goal. During the next year and a half in law school, I interned at MCA and Rhino Records. I passed the California Bar and started temping in the mailroom at Virgin and Sony. But I couldn't get an assistant job anywhere because everyone said that lawyers aren't creative, and I was too ambitious. They felt I could end up taking their jobs."

"You? Ambitious?" Brad said sarcastically.

"So, I started my own music magazine and began writing for some publications like *Billboard*, *Music Connection*, *Hits*, and a bunch of others. I finally got my job at Zomba Publishing after applying to every record label, publisher, and management company from *A* to *Z* in the Yellow Pages of Rock, which was an actual thing back then."

"So how did you meet Brad?" Rob asked.

"That almost didn't happen either," I said.

"Let's rewind a couple years to mid-fall, 1997. 'As Long as You Love Me' was blasting from the corner office. I was rushing out my door, throwing on my black leather jacket as Stephanie yelled, 'Hey, Jeff, Ben on line one!'

"Grabbing the last-minute call, I said, 'What's up, man?'

"'What's up is I got you VIP passes to the Interscope party tonight as my guest. Snoop, Dre, Jimmy Iovine, everyone will be there! Oh, and I heard that chick you like, Tanya, is gonna show, so you better not be late.'

"'Thanks, but I'm giving a lecture at UCLA tonight,' I shouted over the Backstreet Boys demo. 'I'm leaving Zomba right now.'

"'You're gonna choose to lecture some pimply faced kids over Interscope's open bar, sushi, and hot models? You can do your networking thing at the event since that's all you seem to care about. It's a win-win!'

"'Wait. They got free sushi and open bar? I'll try to make it after,' I said, staring at all the plaques lining the hallways. Plaques that weren't mine. 'I need to have some success before I party this job away.'

"As I was throwing on my jacket, approximately four miles away, a young man I'd never met, named Brad Delson, threw a green backpack over his shoulder and headed off to his communication studies class. As he headed down the red brick pathway, he had no idea he'd meet the mysterious guest lecturer: Jeff Blue from Zomba Music Publishing."

"This sounds like an episode of *Twilight Zone*," Joe laughed.

"I blasted the debut album of Limp Bizkit, as I battled traffic up Sunset Boulevard, banging my hands on the steering wheel, trying to drown out the infectious Backstreet melody that was stuck in my head. Sprinting across the campus with less than thirty seconds to spare, I swung the heavy door open, huffing and puffing.

"Professor Marde Gregory smiled, 'Ah, always a grand entrance for one of my favorite students.'

"Waving to the classroom filled with about sixty students, I nervously stepped toward the podium to greet my former professor.

"'Class, I want to introduce you to this gentleman who sat in your seats only eight years ago. He was always very talented and driven, but like most of you,' she said pointing and smiling to certain students in the audience, 'he didn't have any idea what he wanted to do for a career. He was acting in commercials while he interned for Harvey Levin, who's now on TMZ. Harvey told him to go to law school so he could become a news anchor and legal reporter, and through some twists that Jeff, I'm sure, will tell you about, he's now here in front of us. Jeff also teaches classes at UCLA called Artist Development in the Music Industry and Songwriting, both in the UCLA Extension program. Let's give a warm welcome to Jeff Blue.'

"I stepped nervously up to the podium. 'Someone once told me, with the right music, you either forget everything or remember everything. That's power. Now, I am sure you can tell from my appearance, I was never the cool kid,' I spoke over muffled laughter. 'Music allowed me to realize that I wasn't alone. Music says, "It's okay to be the authentic version of me, and if you don't like it, you can F off!" So I made it my career goal to become an A&R executive.'

"A blonde with a sorority sweatshirt raised her hand slowly, 'What exactly is your job? What's A&R?'

"'You know when you see those photos of your favorite band, champagne corks flying in the air while they are holding platinum records? There's always that one out-of-focus guy, peering over their heads. That guy is me. The A&R guy. The "guy" behind the "guy." My job is to find the diamond in the rough, the hidden talent, before anyone else does. Actually, even before the artist knows how good they are. Then sign, develop, and nurture the artist so we can make the world a better place and live happily ever after,' I replied with a smile.

"A curly-haired kid in the front raised his hand. 'What are the most important things outside the obvious hard work that it takes to succeed in the music business?'

"'Well, you need to be present. Not just looking to where you're going, but actually be present in the *now*. You need to be relentless in the pursuit of your passion. You're at a pivotal time in your life where you should be taking every opportunity possible. My introduction to the music business was by complete mistake, around September 1991.'

"I told the class about my fortuitous meeting at Geffen.

"'And now I'm here, at the same class, looking for an intern, who has the unrelenting passion to create something special.'

"Walking over to the PA system, I played a rough demo cassette of a song called 'I Try.' I could see some of the kids' interest fading. 'Any thoughts about this song or the artist?'

"The curly-haired kid glanced around, half raised his hand, and without being called on offered, 'It's not really my style of music, but I like her old-school flow and the minimalist beat. Seems natural, like she's not trying to impress anyone. She has her own sound. I don't know if I like the song or her voice, but it's memorable.'

"'Thanks for your honesty and well-stated opinion. I think her voice has a perfect, let's call it a perfect imperfection, an authentic vulnerability. Thanks for your insight. Maybe you should be an A&R person,' I laughed.

"'What's your artist's name?'

"'Macy Gray. What's your name?'

"'I'm Brad.'

"'Well, thanks, everyone. My hour is up, so I'm leaving a stack of cards on the podium. If anyone is interested in the internship, please reach me at my office.'

"The next morning, head pounding, I stumbled into Zomba at 10:14 with this curly-haired kid in my office chair. He had the strength, vision, and determination to get in the door, and he never left. He's sitting right next to us now. Mister Brad Delson."

CHAPTER 33

BUILDING THE TEAM

ONCE KYLE LEFT THE BAND, BRAD CAME TO THE OFFICE SEEM-ingly concerned.

"We need to find a bass player."

"There's one guy who knows every musician available out there. I can always count on Barry Squire."

"Barry, the A&R guy? He passed on us, didn't he?"

"Yes, but he has a side business."

I picked up the phone. "Hey, Barry, do you have a bassist that can play live but also has the studio chops for Hybrid Theory?"

"I may have a guy. I'll help you for free as a favor, as long as I don't have to go to another rehearsal in that Hollywood room."

"Why's that?" I asked, offended.

"The last time I was there, the pipes were leaking from the ceiling. We were all afraid of being electrocuted!"

"At least it's something to remember the band by. That leak's been remedied."

"As long as I don't get sewage dripped on me, that's fine. I'll send you some tapes of this guy Scott Koziol who could be a good fit."

Rob Bourdon called Scott, had a couple of phone interviews, and invited him down for an audition, but Dave had been part of the original chemistry of the band, and anyone else would always feel like a replacement.

CHAPTER 34

THE DUST BROTHERS

I WAS BATTLING TRAFFIC UP LA CIENEGA TO SUNSET WHEN "Devil's Haircut" by Beck came on KROQ. My good friend Mike Simpson, with his partner John King, produced Beck's *Odelay* album and Beastie Boys' *Paul's Boutique*, and he had an innovative perspective on production, never taking the obvious route. The producer is essential. I didn't need someone who was just a hard rock producer. I wanted someone who first and foremost understood song structure, could write if necessary, and had a firm grip on innovative sound design. I thought they'd be perfect to produce Hybrid Theory. Mike hadn't heard any music since the band was Xero. He was the first call I made when I got to the office.

"Hey, Mike, what are you working on?"

"Jeff, been a minute. We just signed a deal with MCA to do a Dust Brothers album."

"Congrats! That's amazing. Remember that kid, Brad, my intern that played poker with me at your stepdad's condo?"

"I think so. You sent me a demo."

"That's the one. I know you weren't really feeling it, but we have a new singer, new songs, new band name. They're now called Hybrid Theory. You're still A&R at DreamWorks, right?"

"Yup, still there. Lots of irons in the fire," he said. "I'll check it out. You've been working on this forever, so I'm down to hear this new music."

A week later Simpson called me at the office. "I'm blown away. The sound and singer have definitely improved. You all should come over to the studio in Silver Lake."

"I'll be traveling next week, but I'll set it up for you all to meet and see if you gel."

After meeting the following week, Simpson called me in New York. "Just Brad and Mike came. We were hoping to meet your new singer. We played them a lot of tracks. Basic stuff. Like thirty-second loops. They picked out one they liked, so I gave it to them to work on for our album. It was funny, I think my partner was trying to impress your rapper with the new digital mixing board he just got."

"Hilarious. Mike knows a good amount about production and mixing. Was he impressed with John's gear?"

"I don't think so," he laughed. "I can tell Shinoda's an intelligent guy. Before we move forward, I'd like to meet with the singer, too, if that's cool."

The next week, after Simpson met Chester, he called again. "Chester's cool. I'm in to have the guys do a song for our album."

"That would be great, but I'm really looking for a producer for their album. But I want them to have a relationship with you."

"This could be great for both of us. If they do a great job, maybe we can work something out where we produce or mix a song for them."

THE DUST BROTHERS

Mike Shinoda came in the following week with his version of the Dust Brothers track. It had him rapping but was missing Chester's vocals. As I listened, I knew this was more than just a track for the Dust Brothers, this could be a great Hybrid song.

I sent the demo to Mike Simpson who responded immediately. "This is incredible."

I provided Shinoda with the good news, and he and Chester went into the studio and banged out a demo that floored me. I included the song on the EP to potential producers.

CHAPTER 35

MANAGEMENT

It was October 1999, and despite Hybrid Theory having a firm short-form offer from Warner, I couldn't find one manager or producer interested in working with the band. I was at Universal Studios Halloween Horror Night in a maze designed by Rob Zombie. I thanked his manager, Andy Gould, for the tickets, and begged him to reconsider managing the band.

"I've listened to these guys for the past two years, seen them live, hung out at your Zomba Christmas parties with the kids, but I don't get it," Andy said. "Have you thought about Rob McDermott? He just took Static-X gold, and they're at Warner. We should all meet up at the gold-record ceremony next week. He's the only one in our office that likes your band. I think it could be a good match."

Next week I walked with Brad and Mike into the courtyard at 3300 Warner Boulevard in Burbank. Across the crowded gold award presentation, Rob McDermott waved, smiled, and walked over to us.

"Good to see you again," he said, shaking my hand. "Are these the Hybrid guys?" he asked, shaking hands with Brad and

Mike. "I can't stop listening to your demos. I already have strong connections here at Warner, so I know which strings to pull to get things done. They're a great partner. Pros and cons, of course, but it's been fun with Static-X. Is your singer here? That kid has a cool voice."

"No. He's coming back from Arizona, should be here next week."

We set up a meeting at a cafe next to Turner's Liquors off Doheny and Sunset on a warm October day. As Chester walked in, I noticed Rob's face drop.

Chester excused himself to use the restroom before sitting down, and Rob leaned over to me. "This skinny kid with the glasses is not at all what I envisioned as the voice on the demo."

"I know, it's unreal. He's even better live," I replied just as Chester pulled up a seat next to me.

"Nice to meet you, Rob. Jeff has said really great things about you. He doesn't slow down. We hope you have that in common," Chester said.

The conversation ran smoothly until Rob had to leave for a meeting.

"I'm in," Rob said. "Let me know when we can all meet again."

CHAPTER 36

THE PRODUCER

IT WAS EARLY NOVEMBER WHEN I CALLED DANNY HAYES.

"Hey, D! Finding a producer for Hybrid Theory is almost as hard as finding a label. People know we have a deal with Warner, but every current rock producer has passed on working with the band. Did people suddenly become allergic to making money?"

"It's the weirdest thing. I'm getting the same reaction. Even with 'Crawling' and 'Untitled,' people don't think the band has strong-enough songs."

"I sent the demo to Bennett Kaufman, who manages Don Gilmore. He produced Lit and Good Charlotte."

"Those bands aren't anywhere as rock as Hybrid Theory."

"No, but Don clearly understands pop structure and hits. I think he'd be good. I'm waiting to hear."

Don called a few days later. "Hey Jeff. Cool band. I like two of these songs a lot."

"Let me guess, my favorites, 'Untitled' and 'Crawling'?"

"No, this song 'Dust Brothers' and 'Points of Authority.'"

"Really? I think those are both awesome too, but we may have to give the Dust Brothers track to the Dust Brothers for their album."

"I love that song. It's one of the best in the bunch."

"Honestly, Don, I want to make sure we have crossover radio hits that connect with more than just a rock crowd. All the rock these days sounds like a muddy wall of sound. Mike and Joe have so many tasty elements, and I want to hear them all clearly. That's what I like about your production over all the other producers out there now. Clarity," I said emphatically.

"Cool. Let's set up a meeting with you and the band within the next few weeks," Don replied.

With that, I called Simpson, and we agreed that the band would use the song on Hybrid's album as long as Hybrid gave the Dust Brothers a song for their album in the future.

I called Brad with the good news about the track but added, "I like what we have, but we still need at least one undeniably simplistic, no-brainer guitar-riff-driven smash. Think Limp Bizkit's 'Break Stuff' or Green Day's 'Brain Stew.'"

"I know what you mean. Mike and I are working on a couple ideas," Brad said.

CHAPTER 37

THEY HAVE AN OINTMENT FOR THAT

IT WAS NOVEMBER 20, 1999, AND MY BIRTHDAY PARTY WAS packed with music industry execs and artists, including the band. Joe Hahn was talking to my best friend, Lee.

"Congrats on signing to Warner Bros. I've been to a bunch of your showcases and gigs. You're a great DJ."

"Joe's amazing," I said. "He's the glue, the flavor in the mix." Just then, DJ Lethal grabbed me from behind. "Speaking of great DJs," I said. "Good to see you!"

"Happy birthday, Blue! Let's do a shot!" Lethal handed me a shot of tequila and a can of Bud Light.

I introduced Joe to Lethal.

"Hey, Joe, great to meet you. I see you've got the entire mini Limp Bizkit, Hybrid Theory band here," he laughed. "I'm fucking with you. Jeff's played me your music for the last two years. It's really progressing."

Joe smirked. "Great to meet you. I'm a fan. Hey, if you don't mind, I would love some tips, advice, anything you can give me."

"Sure, what's up?"

"I'm having issues with my needle skipping."

"You know they have an ointment for that," Lethal joked.

"For real. Brad and Mike are always jumping on the stage. It drives me crazy. I can't function like that."

"Joe is really percussive," I added. "He has a lot of guitar and synth sounds that he works with. He's not just a DJ, he's a full instrument."

"That's what us *good* DJs do, Jeff," Lethal laughed. "I have some secret tips for you, Joe. Come down to the studio anytime and I'll help with whatever I can."

Just then, the rest of the band came in with Lee and Carmen, holding an ice cream cake and singing happy birthday. Chester's voice rang through the kitchen.

"Make a wish, make a wish!"

"My birthday wish already is coming true. Getting this deal done and starting what I think is going to be an amazing album with Hybrid Theory." Blowing out the candles, I closed my eyes and prayed. It was a great moment.

"I know you love graffiti art and you love the sun, so here you go," Mike said. "I made this painting for you, because you've only been asking me for it for months." He presented me with a canvas of the sun.

"I love your artwork. Thanks so much."

CHAPTER 38

THE VISION

𝕿HE LONG-FORM WARNER CONTRACT WAS STILL BEING FINAL-
ized, and the band was getting anxious about making an album as
they sat in my Zomba office.

"We know you're not officially in the building, but we want to
have a meeting with the heads of each department so they can
understand our vision," Brad said.

"Most bands go through that process after an album is finished, mixed, and mastered, so this is a bit out of the ordinary, but I
agree. It would be a good thing for the label to get to know you and
feel invested before you start recording."

The label meeting was set up. Brad and Mike took center stage
and introduced the band in a professional, businesslike manner,
outlining the band's vision, and demonstrating their intelligence
with a clear musical and artistic direction. The execs looked
around at one another as they flipped through the band's outline.
As the guys departed to meet with the head of the art department,

I heard one say, "If we're going to be taking direction from a *band*, they better be good."

A few days later, a friend who worked at EMI, Matt Messer, held his birthday party at El Compadre. Some A&R VIPs motioned me over to their group, and a large guy leaned in and said, "Listen, you haven't even started at Warner and you and your band are already making enemies." I could smell the alcohol on his breath.

"This is a joke, right?"

"You shopped Hybrid Theory for three years and now you dump them on Warner Bros. You told the art department that the band wants to create their own artwork."

"The band has two amazing artists in it, *both* of whom went to art school. They're just expressing their vision. We just had a meeting with the entire label, and the execs seemed to like them," I replied.

"The band should be listening to the execs who have the proven track record instead of shoving them down everyone's throat before you've even started making an album. Control your band. I'm trying to help you," he slurred.

"The band is very excited to be there, and they're smart guys. No one is intentionally disrespecting anyone or their experience, so I'm sorry if it came off that way, but I'm not going to apologize for the band having an authentic vision. I won't even officially be in the building for another four months, so thanks for the heads-up," I said, slightly shaking from the ambush.

"Just be careful. You worked hard to get this job, but your career could be short if you don't listen to the people that have been there," he said, looming over me with a drink in his hand. "Let Melanie do her job. She's the head of the art department for a reason."

His buddy, the same VP of A&R at Columbia that passed on the band two months before, laughed as I absorbed the verbal assault.

He placed his hand on my shoulder and said, "Looks like you may have the shortest A&R career ever."

I was visibly confused and angry and, at the same time, fearful that I had allowed the band too much freedom. It was my first A&R job, and I was thrown in at the top. He was correct. I did need to listen to those above me. At Zomba, my bosses, Neil and Richard, allowed me to make my own creative decisions, but at a major label, there were real politics, egos, and agendas to deal with. There was a chain of command where executives got fired with every new regime change. I didn't want to be a casualty. I went outside and dialed Mike's number.

"You won't believe what just happened. I just got chewed out at a party. I was told we need to back off the art department."

"Back off from what? Giving our ideas about our artwork? I'm not going to back off, and neither should you. I don't really need to hear these negative things."

"I agree and I support whatever you want. I just promised to tell you everything so there are no surprises."

CHAPTER 39

DROPPING LIKE FLIES

AFTER MONTHS OF NEGOTIATING, ON DECEMBER 10 THE final Warner long-form contracts arrived. The band signed, and it was official. They had been advised to hold off signing a management contract until after their label deal was signed so they wouldn't have to pay a commission on their advance.

Rob McDermott, waiting in the wings, called to ask what was taking them so long.

"They took nine months to do my publishing deal and a couple months to decide on Chester. It's crazy. I'll push to get it done."

The band finally decided to hire Rob as their manager in early February 2000, and I wasted no time greeting him.

"Welcome aboard," I told him. "We start recording next month at NRG."

"This is moving quickly," he replied with his signature laugh. "I'm excited. You make sure the radio guys get their hits, and I'll spend my time finding tours and giving the band ideas to build their street cred and fan base."

A few weeks later on February 28, 2000, at ten in the morning, the phone rang. It was Joe McEwen. He was always so positive and relaxed, but there was a different tone in his voice today. "I just wanted to let you know that Phil Quartararo, our president, is going to be taking over a lot of Russ's duties. I know Russ was a big reason you chose Warner Bros. He's still around, but I'm not sure for how much longer. He really liked you. I'm sorry."

"At least you're still there," I replied.

"I'm not going anywhere. I'm sure you're getting ready to make the album, so if you need anything, let me know. I've got your back."

Eight days later, on March 8, Joe called again. This time his voice was even more distressed. "It's Joe McEwen, dude." He never called me dude, and it sounded odd coming from him. "I have some news. I've been demoted, and David Kahne is the new head of A&R for all of Warner. There's been a regime change."

"What? David passed on Hybrid three times. The two reasons I came to Warner Bros. are you and Russ, and neither of you is going to be there when I finally arrive?"

I hung up the phone. My stomach was twisting in knots as Ariana entered the room with a rolled-up magazine.

"What are you doing?"

"This friggin' fly is driving me crazy," she said as the fly landed on my desk. *Splat.* The fly's guts spilled on my fake-wood-paneled desk as the phone rang.

"Jeff Blue's office," Ariana said. Then, handing me the phone, she told me, "It's David Kahne for you."

I gulped, staring at the smashed fly. "Hello, David."

"Good morning. I'm not sure if you heard yet, but I'm the new head of A&R at Warner."

"Congratulations!" I said trying to sound surprised and excited.

"I want to talk to you about you and your band, Hybrid Theory. Let's grab lunch this week in Burbank."

"Okay. Is there something wrong?"

"No, not really. Let's just meet and discuss in person. Also, please send me the band's newest music."

"Okay. I think they have a few hits. I'm sending a CD over now."

I sat down in my green chair, head in hands, the fly's dead eyes staring back at me. *I hope this isn't a sign,* I thought to myself.

Later that week, David and I sat in a booth, staring blankly at our menus while a waitress brought us drinks. Swishing his straw around his iced tea, he abruptly said, "So, I know we've met at some of the Hybrid rehearsals, but I want to get to know you a bit more. To start off with, congrats on starting soon. What do you think your strengths are? Specifically, what qualifies you to do A&R?"

"I'm forward thinking, I write and play three instruments, I can relate to artists on a variety of levels. I signed Macy, who was just nominated for a Grammy for Best New Artist." Stopping with a nervous laugh, I said, "Wait, is this an interview? Aren't I already hired? I start in a few days."

"I'm just trying to get the lay of the land here. And, yes, I know," he added. "I wouldn't have signed her, but congratulations on her success."

I laughed uncomfortably.

"Of course, your deal is done. But Joe's not in charge of A&R anymore. I've seen Hybrid Theory two or three times now," he said, folding his hands on the table. "You think they're ready to make an album?"

"Did you hear the demos I sent over? 'Untitled' or 'In the End' and 'Crawling,' I think there's some really good songs on there. Don't you?"

"I don't hear a single. But they're signed now, so..."

Time seemed to move in slow motion as I stared at my Diet Coke, the condensation slowly dripping down the sides of the glass, pooling around the waxed wood table, creating a ring. My head was spinning. I couldn't listen to any more doom and gloom. I knew right then and there I had to move quickly or the band, myself, or both could be dropped before we entered the building on March 24. I set up a meeting with marketing director Peter Standish and I called Brad.

"How's that first single coming along?"

"The face-melter? We're working on it. What's up? You sound stressed."

"Joe McEwen is gone. Russ is also gone."

"What happened?"

"David Kahne happened. He's my new boss!"

"You're joking." He laughed nervously. "I can never tell with you. Are you being serious? The guy passed on us three times."

"I am. Don't freak out. I'm going to make an appointment with Peter Standish, the marketing director, to get things moving. Just come up with an undeniable smash track." After hanging up the phone with Brad, I dialed the marketing department.

The marketing director holds the incredibly important job of coordinating the details of all departments, along with the A&R exec, to move a project from inception to release, and organizing an overall schedule and budget for the label to work with. I entered the large Warner lobby, registered with security, and introduced myself as the new VP of A&R. Once in his office, Peter, a tall, thin, congenial guy who seemed like a straight shooter, greeted me with a smile.

"Welcome to the building," he said. "A lot of changes happening around here." He motioned for me to sit down in a chair opposite him as he flipped through some papers. "It looks like we are tentatively scheduled for an album release date of mid-August 2000."

"August? That's in four months! We don't even know what songs are going to be on the album, let alone beginning to record it! Rob McDermott just signed on to manage the band. We were thinking we could get an EP, even some promo cassettes, anything to build street credibility while we're making the album."

"We can do that," Peter smiled.

"Cool. It's important that the band presents this as an indie release to keep street cred, which would mean we really don't want any mention of Warner Bros. on the artwork or packaging. Not even the Warner logo. Plus, the band is visually driven, so Mike and Joe want as much control over the art as possible."

"Not having a WB logo may get tricky, but I get what you're saying. I'll run it by legal." Peter stood up and shook my hand. His chill demeanor put me at ease, and I was glad he was on our team.

CHAPTER 40

SHOULDN'T YOU BE ON VACATION?

NEIL PORTNOW WALKED INTO MY OFFICE. "HEY, MR. WORK-aholic, don't you want to take a few vacation days before you start at Warner Bros.?" he asked me. "You know it's going be a lot more pressure than it is around here."

"The band's showing up in a few minutes with some new songs. I can't wait."

Just then Mike and Brad arrived. Mike sat down at my Pearl drum set as Brad threw a disk with Hybrid Theory written in black sharpie into the CD player. My face lit up like a firework as he blasted one of the most instantly memorable guitar hooks I had heard in a long time. It was titled "Plaster." The signature "One Step Closer" riff came blasting through my speakers. The next song idea was a guitar line for "Papercut." I couldn't stop smiling. They were rough guitar and beat ideas, but I could immediately tell they were going to be big. I had an especially good feeling about "Plaster."

SHOULDN'T YOU BE ON VACATION?

A colleague in the neighboring office screamed, "Turn it down! I can't hear myself think!"

In response to my neighbor's request, I played the songs again, turning up the stereo so loud I could feel the walls shake. Neil walked by my office, smiled, and give us a thumbs-up. "Play it as loud as you want!" Neil shouted. "I'm happy for all of you."

"I fucking love you guys! This finally sounds like a band you can call Hybrid Theory," I screamed as I hit my hands on the desk to the beat of the drums.

"Are we ready to record?" Brad asked.

"Fuck yes, you are! NRG studios in North Hollywood. Let's make a hit album."

On March 7, 2000, we drove to the parking lot on 11128 Weddington Street and parked inside the gates. Walking into the lobby with cement floors and candy in glass jars, an assistant greeted us and took us back to Don Gilmore in the studio area. The lounge was filled with rugs hanging from the ceiling, a pool table, game area, and a freshly stocked fridge in the private studio green room. "This is it, guys, your new home for the next month and a half. This is where you're going to make magic."

Don entered and we all shook hands. He gave us the lay of the land, showed us the main room, recording bay, and all the gear, while an assistant was setting up the two-inch tape.

"I love the sound in this studio," I told Don. "How was recording the other bands in here?"

"I think the guys would love what went down with the last band. We had hookers doing blow off each other's tits. It was pure rock 'n' roll decadence."

"That won't fly with Hybrid. They're strictly business, definitely no strippers. Just the music with no distractions. "

ONE STEP CLOSER

The wheels were in motion. On March 13, Drum Doctors unloaded drums, hardware, and cymbals for Rob. Everything was tuned and ready to go the following day.

Rob began recording drums at noon on the fourteenth and finished at one in the morning, smashing through "Harmonic Song," "Pictureboard," "By Myself," "Plaster," "Papercut," "Rhinestone (Forgotten)," and "And One." The next day, he laid down tracks for "Untitled," "Esaul (A Place for My Head)," "Dust Bros.," and "Stick 'n' Move." Day three was spent finishing "Stick 'n' Move," "Slip," and "A Place for My Head." Day four rounded out "Points of Authority," "Pushing Me Away," and "Now I See."

Friday, March 24, the band came to my new office for the first time.

"Nice spot, man!" they said.

"Look at this insane desk I got from Jimmy in the storage room."

"It looks like a '70s airplane," Chester said. "You don't want something new?"

"I was told that this was Ted Templeman's desk. Van Halen, the Doobie Brothers. Some legendary shit went down at this desk," I said, as I opened the top drawer. Something rattled inside. I reached in and pulled out a penny. Kissing the copper piece, I said, "Good luck," and taped it to the inside of the desk. "This is going to be an amazing year!"

Over the next two weeks, the tracks evolved tremendously, but a large number of lyrics and melodies remained unfinished. As I entered the lounge, Brad grabbed a piece of fruit, while Mike hovered over the pool table and slid the eight ball into the corner pocket without a stick.

Taking the last bite of a banana, Brad said, "We're just discussing lyrics and curse words. It seems like every band has a parental warning sticker for profanity."

With Mark and Brad at the Zomba Christmas Party, 1997.

Zomba Christmas Party 1998 (L to R): Steve Plinio, Brad, Dave, me, Mark, Danny Hayes, Rob, Scott Harrington, and Joe.

Taken after signing the publishing deal, 1998. (L to R): Danny Hayes, Mike, Rob, Joe, Mark, Brad, and me.

Chester rehearsing the Xero songs prior to leaving for LA. Arizona, 1999.

Fourth of July, 2000, with Mike and Joe, and smoking a cigar with Chester.

Vegas, 2000, with (top) Rob Bourdon, Rob Goldklang, Chester, Rob McDermott, Scott, (bottom) Monroe Grisman, me, Mike, and Myra Simpson.

Wearing the original Hybrid Theory tee shirt and raising a toast with Mike, Monroe Grisman, and Rob Goldklang, Vegas, 2000.

Mike and Chester with the Deftones.

Live 105 Radio Interview, 2000.

(PHOTOS COURTESY OF SAMANTHA BENNINGTON)

(Photos courtesy of Samantha Bennington)

Celebrating my birthday with the band and Lee and Sayuri Lubin, November, 1999.

With Joe, Danny Hayes, and Brad at Lee Lubin's birthday, January, 2000.

Chester in his backyard, April, 2000.

Chester with Draven on the tour bus, 2002.

Carmen and Samantha, Halloween.

Chester backstage at Ozzfest, 2000.

(PHOTO COURTESY OF
SAMANTHA BENNINGTON)

Celebrating Linkin Park's first Gold album, Sacramento, 2000.

SHOULDN'T YOU BE ON VACATION?

Mike played with the pool cue. "Our music should be powerful enough to send our message without cussing. I don't want it filled with 'fuck this' and 'fuck that.'"

"Almost every rock album has a sticker. It makes kids want to buy the album as a 'fuck you' to parents," I responded, nevertheless intrigued by the concept. I moved over to Chester, who was sitting down at the table writing and looking up occasionally. I glanced at his words and was struck by their power. "Guys, you're bringing in the new millennium as arbiters of the new zeitgeist and can have a real impact on this generation."

Joe laughed, "In English, please?"

Chester turned to me, "Zeit...what?"

Brad chimed in, "We have the opportunity to say and stand for something important for the new decade." He paused for a moment before continuing.

"Not just the decade but more. Anything you put out into the universe has the potential to affect generations. There's two angles here. It has been shown that having a sticker incentivizes kids to buy the album, but, your performance, your energy and intensity should make a kid in his Ohio basement feel like screaming 'fuck' when they hear your music."

Mike finished his thought, "And then you've got them hooked much deeper than if we actually have to say the words ourselves. So," Mike said as he stood with the pool cue, "we're all okay with no cursing?"

"Zeitgeist...I like it," Chester said.

"Good. It's settled. No cursing."

In the parking lot I dialed two A&R friends to ask if they could think of a recent rock album that didn't have a parental advisory sticker. They couldn't. I was impressed with the forward-thinking creative and business decisions the band was making. They didn't rely on gimmicks. It was all substance.

A few says later at the studio, Don and I were reviewing the tracks.

"I want these songs to be short," I told him. "Every second should serve a purpose. Let's trim the fat and leave the listener wanting more."

I began writing detailed notes on each song on a yellow legal pad and handed them to Don.

"I know the guys love this part," he said, pointing to page five of my notes.

"So do I, but it's incongruent. Guide them to create better transitions. You're doing a great job, Don. Thanks"

Just then Chester walked into the room and sat at the control board. He put his hand on the back of his neck. "Man, can you imagine going gold?"

Brad opened the door at that moment and said, "Let's shoot for two hundred fifty thousand first."

Chester looked at me as if he wanted to say something but just laughed.

Later that evening, Samantha, Chester, and I went for dinner across the street at Tokyo Delve's Rockin' Sushi. I could tell something was bothering him.

"I've known you long enough to sense when something's on your mind. What's up?"

"I'm not sure, but there's just some weirdness," he said, sipping his miso soup. "I'm not sure what's going on in their heads, but your position, jumping from our publisher to our A&R guy, is an issue. Your role used to be, 'Hey, guys, I'm here to support you, great job, rah rah.' Now it's like, 'Guys, this doesn't work. Change this, I like this, I don't like that.' You're way more critical. They think you're micromanaging the album, focusing more on my vocals and the rock sound as opposed to the hip hop. They just feel you're wearing too many hats, and maybe a little too controlling."

"That's really disappointing to hear. What about you? How's your relationship with the band?" I asked.

"I don't know."

"I'm sure you're fine, Chester."

"There's kind of an outsider vibe," Samantha added. "Probably because he's the new guy."

"It's true. Other than you, the only person I hang with is Scott. I feel like the band thinks they need to babysit me. They're worried I'm going to start drinking and smoking."

"Well, you've got a glass of beer, a shot of sake in your hand, which you're about to drop in the beer, and that blunt I know you have in your car, which you're gonna smoke later," I said, laughing. "That's not an irrational feeling for the band to have. How's the living situation?"

"It sucks. I'm back and forth from Santa Clarita. It's a long drive to NRG, but I don't care. I'll sleep in the car—I'll do whatever it takes."

"Well, definitely watch the drugs and alcohol. I've never seen a band this straight and narrow, but it could possibly be the one thing that drives the success above and beyond the music. We should respect that."

"For sure. By the way, are you and Carmen okay?" Chester asked.

"Yeah, I think so."

"Wrong, honey. Carmen isn't happy with you in the studio all the time," Samantha said. "She's been talking to me. Just a heads-up."

"Wow, all this good news," I said sarcastically. My head started spinning from exhaustion as I dramatically bit the head off a deep fried shrimp.

"I just want you to know," Chester paused dramatically, "Samantha and I appreciate everything you've done. We are here for you, *but*, just in case shit gets weird, I need to always take the band's side. I'm trying to be a team player as much as I can. I hope you understand that."

"So, basically, you're saying my wife and the band are upset with me. I'm going to head home and sleep on the couch with the dogs. They'll be happy to see me." I paused. "Or are they upset too?"

The following Monday, Rob McDermott said he wanted to meet with the band and me at NRG. I entered the studio in a good mood, my jacket covered in dog hair. The band and manager were on one side of the lounge, facing me, and we exchanged laughs for a brief moment.

Out of nowhere, Rob said, "Hey, we have an issue. The band needs more money in the budget for food. Warner can't expect the band to be creative with this small of a food budget."

"This is the exact budget you asked for. The label administration had to sign off. I can't just go change it. Plus, the guys have plenty of food. They order from the menu book all day long," I said, pointing at the huge binder of menus. "Are you joking?"

Suddenly Rob got really angry and yelled, "No, I'm serious. Go do your job. Warner Bros. isn't respecting the band, and they want more money for food!"

"Maybe you're eating half the food. You seem to have gained a shit-ton of weight, man. Maybe it's time for a diet," I laughed. "Rob, let me speak to you in private."

Walking down to the middle of the concrete floored hall, I said quietly in an intense whisper that reverberated through the corridor, "What the hell are you doing, man? What's with throwing a shit-fit?"

"I've just gotta show the band that I've got balls. They know I was just fucking with you. I was joking. Kind of."

"Didn't feel like you were joking. When you use that tone, it makes it seem like you don't respect me or the label, like we don't get along. We should all be on the same team. I've been with these guys since the beginning, so I don't want to be on opposing sides or play games."

"Sorry, man, I didn't mean for it to look that way. We are on the same team. But I told the band to keep you and the label at a distance. I need to be the asshole now, and everything should go through me. I agree that all the changes you're suggesting are making it better. But maybe don't be so direct. Let them think they came up with the ideas on their own."

I walked down the hall, feeling the foreboding "band vs. record label" myth becoming a reality. If I wasn't already the enemy, I was about to become one.

"Hey," Rob caught up to me as I was entering my car. "Do I really need to lose that much weight?"

I slammed the door and threw the car into reverse, exiting the parking lot with a rush. I should have taken that vacation.

CHAPTER 41

ONE STEP BACK

I SAT IN MY OFFICE ON A MONDAY, THINKING A MONTH EAR-lier, everything seemed to be moving in the right direction. Everybody seemed to be on the same page. Now, in early April, my boss and main supporter were out of the picture, the band was feeling like I was overwhelming them, and my home life was crumbling. Things seemed to be on the verge of going off the rails. Just then, Ariana buzzed my office.

"David Kahne is on the line," she said. "I'm putting him through."

I choked on my Diet Coke, and the bubbles burned in my nose. I felt like I was always walking on eggshells with him.

"How's the album going?" he asked.

"It's awesome. The band is working their asses off writing as they record, and I feel like they have three or four potential hits," I said.

"Great. I'll come down today to check out what you have so far. How's three o'clock?"

"The guys are a little sensitive about people being in the studio. It's mainly scratch vocals. I'd rather give them a little more time before you listen."

"Okay. I'll come down at five."

"I meant more days, not hours...," I said.

"I know what you meant," he laughed. "I'll see you at six."

Perfect, I thought. *Thanks for the additional time.*

"Three hits...," I heard him mutter as he hung up.

I called the studio, tapping my pen on my desk until Don answered. I explained that David was coming by and that we needed to play the best songs we had.

"That's okay, he's the boss."

The bowl of Honey Nut Cheerios I'd had that morning was acid-refluxing its way up my throat as I entered NRG. I pushed open the heavy studio door and saw the guys nervously sitting around the console with Don. They looked relieved that I was alone.

"Just me, guys. David should be here in twenty or so. No one be nervous."

"We aren't nervous. He's going to love it!" Mike said with a smile.

Before I could say another word, the heavy door swung open and David stood in the doorway, looking ominous.

"Looks like the right place," he smiled in his white polo shirt. "Good to see you all again. Jeff tells me you guys have some hits here."

"You want to hear what we've got so far?" Don asked, standing up to give David his seat at the board. "You want to hear it through the NS10s or the big monitors?"

"I got it from here, thanks," David replied as he pressed the space bar and the songs began to thunder through the massive studio speakers. I was impressed the great work Don and the band

167

had accomplished as I glanced through my peripheral vision at David, who didn't display any emotion while he listened.

Into the fourth song, he leaned into the middle of the console as if he were concentrating. Halfway into the song, he leaned back and rubbed his temples, hitting the pause button. Swiveling around in the chair, he paused. "Thank you, guys. I'm glad I came down."

"I appreciate you letting me listen at this stage in the process. Jeff, you want to walk with me to the car?"

Following his lead out to the parking lot, the contrast from the dark studio to the bright sun stung my eyes. He turned to me and stated, "I'm torn. The songs I just heard aren't hits yet, but they have the potential. That kid Chester can sing, but what are you going to do about the rapper?"

"What do you mean?"

Shrugging his shoulders, he tossed the CD onto the passenger seat and said, "Let me think about this. Meet me in my office tomorrow at four."

At 3:57 p.m. Wednesday I climbed the stairs into his office, where his assistant, Crystal, directed me to sit down across from him.

"Look," he said. "The good news is that kid Chester has an amazing voice."

"What's the bad news?"

"The rapper doesn't. There's a reason you didn't get any offers on the band before. Does the rapper do any writing other than his rapping?"

"He does a ton. He basically produces and writes at least fifty to sixty percent of everything, maybe more. I honestly didn't even realize how much until recently."

"Can you talk to him? Get him to take a step back?"

"What do you mean step back?"

"He's not a great rapper. He's sounds so pedestrian. Anything he does minimizes the impact of Chester's vocals, which is the strength of the band."

"I don't know what to say," I said in shock.

"I figured as much, but luckily I have a solution. I just spoke to Mad Lion. You know who that is, right?"

"Of course," I lied, trying not to seem stupid. "Cool band."

"You don't have to lie to me, Jeff. Mad Lion is a rapper, not a band. He's worked with me on Sublime, KRS-One, Biggie. He's amazing. I spoke to him, and he's into rapping on some of the tracks and possibly even replacing Mike."

"You spoke to another rapper?" I said, my mouth dropping open. "You can't do that. Mike's essential to the band's sound and direction."

"You replaced the original singer, didn't you? Talk to the guys. I can tell they're smart, and they'll know what's best for their band. I know you've put years of work into the band and don't want to see them dropped, so it's..."

"Dropped?" I said, shaking my head in disbelief. It felt like he was looking for ways to derail my psyche.

With a motion of his hand, as if he were clearing the air, he said, "Let's not jump the gun. Just suggest Mad Lion. See what they say. I'm also okay with not having a rapper. Chester can hold the vocals on his own. I have no problem with Mike writing."

My breathing became shallow. "I'm totally confused. What makes this band different than anything else is the amazing chemistry between Chester and Mike. Call and response with two front men. It's unlike anything out there."

"They're not doing anything that hasn't been done a dozen times before. Just make sure you talk to them before they record anything else," he said, cutting me off.

CHAPTER 42

KILL THE MESSENGER

DRIVING TO THE STUDIO TO DELIVER THE NEWS, I FOUND DON standing over Chester at the computer in the lounge. Brad was in the kitchen and I motioned to him. "Hey, look, I need to ask you something. Not sure what other way to say this, but..."

"You look like you've seen a ghost," Brad said in his calming voice, a smile crossing his face. "It's okay, what's up?"

"David said he loves Chester, thinks we've got some good songs. But..."

"But what?"

"But he wants to replace Mike."

"Get rid of Mike?" He was trying to absorb what I had said and was silent for a few seconds. "Do you know how ridiculous that sounds? You know there's absolutely no way that's happening."

"I'm just telling you what he said. He suggested some guy named Mad Lion? And he wants to make Mike more of a writer."

"What?" Breathing heavily, he paused and collected his thoughts. Then, in his most calming voice, he said, "You need to tell the band this." He left the room for a few minutes, which felt like hours, and finally returned with the group.

Hungry, dizzy, and ill-prepared for a full band dialogue, my heart began to race. As I spoke, I could feel the heat of negative energy in the room and realized that this very moment was the beginning of something bad. It was like time moved backward into a whirlpool, and I was caught in it. With every word, a hole was dug deeper, until I felt immersed in dirt, unable to breathe. Mike looked sick, afraid, angry, and sad, all at the same time.

"How could you do this? I built this band. You want to kick me out? There's no way," Mike unleashed. "Couldn't you have my back?"

Someone said, "You want Mad Lion to replace Mike?!"

"First of all, I have no idea who Mad Lion is. I swear. It was David's suggestion. He said he worked with him on some albums. Of course, I have your back!"

"But you said you want Mike out," Brad stated.

"No. This is all getting twisted." I held up my hand, counting on my fingers, "Number one, I signed the band to a publishing deal with Mike as a main writer and producer. Number two, I shopped the band for two and a half years, always supporting Mike, even when people talked shit, and number three," I thrust my hand in the air, "I made it a requirement that anywhere I landed for a job would require me signing the band, with Mike clearly as a front man. So how does this even make the slightest bit of sense that I'd want Mike out? I put my job on the line for you guys, and I don't want to see you shelved or dropped."

"Dropped?" someone in the band said, as they looked at each other with fear and anger.

Suddenly, I realized I should have let McDermott or Danny Hayes deal with this issue. "Trust me, this is not how I envisioned things going at all. Things were different with Joe McEwen, but we have a new head of A&R right now, who's an award winning producer, and giving us direction. You guys are like family, so..."

"Man, this isn't a family. You went from our publisher to our A&R guy. You work for the label now. Not for us."

"That hurts. I've been helping develop the band since your first show. I'm in this because I believe in you individually and as a band. Your songs have the power to say what most people can't express, and I want the world to hear your message. Yes, I work for the label, and although things seemed fucked, the label has the power to get your songs heard by the world."

"We can get another label. There are plenty of record companies that would want us."

"Did you guys just somehow forget the last forty-four rejections? I sure haven't. I hit up every single A&R person from every record label, which means we were passed on by at least six people per label. Let's start with the indies that passed. Red Ant, Capricorn, Epitaph, DV8, Lava, Radioactive, DreamWorks, Elektra, Atlantic, Warner Bros., Reprise, Arista, RCA, Interscope, Flawless, Universal, Universal Republic, Capitol three times, Virgin, Disney, Hollywood Records, A&M, MCA, Island Def Jam, Mercury, American Recordings, Columbia. This is just off the top of my head. If you think there's someone out there that has a new job and will re-sign a band that no one wanted, and on top of that, a band who just walked out of a contract from a major label, then good luck."

"We've got our songs. We can put them out ourselves."

The conversation spiraled out of control in a way I hadn't imagined. "You guys are aware that Warner owns whatever you've done here and in the past, plus there's always a re-recording restriction that would prohibit you from recording any of these songs for any other label for probably like five to ten years, period, if you leave, or even if they drop you. We'd have to start all over again. I know no one wants that."

"What? If we leave or get dropped, we can't take our songs? This is so screwed."

Taking a deep breath, expressing myself as sympathetically as possible, I said, "Guys, first of all, a re-recording restriction is in every single contract no matter where you sign. Second of all, let's not jump the gun. We're a team. I brought this up to Brad to figure out how to deal with it, not start world war three. I won't let anyone get dropped."

"We are a band, so this involves us all," Brad responded. "And I'm sorry, but this," he said, motioning to me on one side and the band on the other, "doesn't feel like a team. At least not anymore."

"*Wow*. I risked everything to get you guys a deal, so don't tell me I'm not part of the team. Do you know how many bands would kill to have your spot right now on a major label? Do you know how many people would kill to have my job? Seriously, let's take a breath. We *are* a team. We got here *together,* but we have different jobs that are *both* on the line. We're all in the same boat that's either going to sink or float, so let's not allow someone to take our jobs."

The band looked like they were exhausted. "Then stand up for us."

"I am standing up for you. Just because we have a record deal, doesn't mean we're invincible. My instinct has gotten us this far, and my instinct tells me that David is at least *somewhat* right."

Mike looked up at me, shaking his head. I knew I had lost his support and friendship at that moment. I was sinking, reacting to what my boss was telling me, unable to balance the needs of the artist, and losing touch with my own instinct. I'd been backed into corner. My heart was in the right place, but the words and my delivery were all wrong. Rookie mistake

"This isn't the end of the world. It just means we need to be stronger. David is a pro, and he has a point. Don's mentioned it to me, too. We're all trying to help."

The room felt claustrophobic. No one spoke, and I stupidly kept talking.

"Come on, Mike, you know the rapping could be better. Listen to some of your early demos. You had this killer flow and energy. Now it sounds too safe and sterile, trying too hard. You know you can do better."

Still no one responded, and I felt the air being sucked out of the room like I was in a vacuum.

"Just give us some space, Jeff," Brad said.

CHAPTER 43

THE BATHROOM FLOOR

IT WAS AN HOUR AND A HALF LATER, AND THE STRESS HAD ME dizzy. I managed to drive home, and now I was straddling the sink, looking in the mirror. I didn't like what I saw, an empty shell of a face struggling to become visible in a life of invisibility.

How had I really expected that to go? I should have waited instead of acting on my boss's orders. Things started to spiral. Cloudy and dark energy swam through my head, as the buildup of self-loathing came to a peak. My body melted to the floor, and memories from six years past came flooding back of me on the bathroom floor of my parents' house. It was late 1994, and I was working–six days a week in the legal department for the Small Business Administration, writing articles and reviews for five music publications, and managing and playing in a band. This particular evening, my parents were yelling at me through the door, calling me a failure, and an embarrassment to their friends. My girlfriend's billionaire father had convinced her to dump me that day. My self-worth and passion were crushed, and I was drowning in self-pity.

Then it hit me. I stood up and looked in the mirror of my parents' bathroom. *Fuck this. Fuck you, Jeff. Stand your ass up off the floor and don't give up. Music is your motivation to live, and you are going to get a fucking job in the music business. You're not a dreamer and fuck anyone who stands in your way.* That second, I felt positive energy rush through me. Being so close to the edge and turning back gave me a renewed purpose and excitement to move forward with my life. But I knew I couldn't stop the momentum and fall back into depression, so I doubled my efforts. A week later I was blessed with a job in an entertainment law firm, and two months after that, I was working at Zomba.

Now it was 2000, only six years later, and my head was swimming in the same dark waters when my mom called. I reluctantly picked up the phone.

"Hey, Mom. Wow, you caught me at a bad time." I explained the situation I was in with Mike, the band, and my boss, David.

"Honey, I wasn't there. But I can tell you this. When you're criticizing an aspect of a band, or individual, regardless if they are open to it, you are attacking their identity. You can't control how someone is going to react. The only thing you *can* control is yourself and how you speak to people. Maybe you were a little harder than you realize. Unfortunately, you're the messenger, and this could lead to them isolating you, and maybe even not trusting you."

"Way to make me feel better, Mom."

"I'm just saying. I know how much you love that kid Brad. And Chester. They know you love them. You'll figure it out. Love you."

"I know. Love you, too."

THE BATHROOM FLOOR

I didn't sleep that night. My brain ran in circles, my body twisted and turned, replaying the events and possible alternatives in every form. It was nine in the morning when my cell rang.

"Jeff, what the fuck?" McDermott chuckled. "I spoke to Kahne about Mike's performance a couple days ago. I knew he was talking about replacing him, but I figured you would at least call me before speaking to the band. We could have spoken to them together, but now you're in the middle of this mega-shitstorm. The band is freaking out that they're going to get dropped."

"The band should know this isn't coming from me. I'm doing what my boss asked me to do."

"We both know David's not entirely wrong. I talked to the guys. They know Mike needs work, but the harder you push, the more they resent you. I explained you're just doing your job, but they are pissed."

"What should I do?"

"What I've learned as a manager is that when we have an idea that we want the band or anyone to execute, it's our job to make it feel like they came up with the idea themselves. Give it a couple days, and we'll think of something. Talk to Chester. Maybe he can help."

Chester and Samantha came over for dinner that Sunday. Shaking my head, I cracked open a couple of cold Coronas and handed him one. We sat around the table before I finally asked him what I should do.

Chester leaned forward. "You're kind of in a fucked position. It seems like originally there was a little bit of a power struggle with Mike and Don Gilmore in the studio. Now that that's chilled out, Mike has to deal with the pressure of you and the head of A&R being upset with his performance. It's really turned the band against you. The fucked-up thing is that ironically, this whole mess is bringing us together as a band. Band against label, ya know?"

"I handled this all wrong. There's so many moving parts. I'm trying to please everyone, and I'm ending up pleasing no one. I should just trust my gut instinct, which is to believe in the band like I have from the beginning. The difference is, I always knew we had time to get the songs better because the band was always in demo phase, and we had plenty of time, preparing for the future when we'd actually be in the studio. But we're in the studio now, making the major label album. Perfection is the only option. There is no more time. The reality is, here we are, and there are some things that need work, but we'll get through it. I've just got to figure out how to maneuver through all the politics," I said, rubbing my forehead. "We gotta keep Mike."

Taking a swig of beer, Chester added, "I know you've had Mike's back from day one and want what's best for us. David just brought up what we all knew was an issue. You could have talked to McDermott and presented it in a more productive way, though. But I know you, and I see the stress you're under. It's eating you alive"

"David's intentions are good, but lots of times, executives get involved who don't know the history, or the chemistry, that makes a group work. There's got to be a good compromise where we get what we want. Maybe we can tell David that Mike will be on fifty percent of the album, and then when we actually record, Mike will be on all of it. We turn the album in, and if we make the album great enough it won't matter."

"I can live with that. Aside from this drama, how are you doing?"

"Fuckin' living the dream. My bedroom is located part-time in a green Toyota Tercel. Rock star life."

"This will all be over soon. You and Samantha should look for a permanent apartment."

With another swig of beer, we threw burgers on the grill and enjoyed the balmy Los Angeles weather with our wives. I felt a weight temporarily lifted.

CHAPTER 44

WE'RE THE PROBLEM

That Monday morning, David asked me up to his office. "How'd the conversations go?" he asked, his head buried in his computer.

"They won't budge. They won't replace Mike, and I agree with them."

He looked up. "Didn't you have this issue with that original singer I saw? That guy was holding the band back, and you replaced him. Clearly you knew what was best for them then, so why are they giving you a problem now?"

"David, they aren't giving me a problem—*we're* giving them the problem by disrupting their chemistry. It's a totally different situation. Mark wasn't right for the band. In this situation Mike *is* half the band. If you take Mike out of the picture, the energy, the writing, the trust and leadership, all of it falls away."

"This is kind of your fault," he replied.

My chest tightened, my breath got shallow, and I saw stars. I felt like I was having a heart attack.

David continued, "You get someone as good as Chester, and it makes everything else pale in comparison, especially a second front man."

I sank into the sofa.

"Are you okay?" he asked as I tried to slow my breathing.

"I just need to eat," I said. "When we replaced Mark, I told the guys if we found the missing element, that it would throw a spotlight on everything. Now it seems the spotlight is focused on Mike."

Nodding his head, David sighed. "Here's the solution. Mike can co-write, play keyboards or guitar, background vocals, whatever, but we have Mad Lion, or someone else, rap. Or we have no rapper and let Chester carry the band."

My head fell into my hands. I sighed. "That won't work."

"Did you speak to Chester?"

"I did and he agrees with me, but he understands what you're concerned about. So, he came up with a solution."

"Oh, good. What's this solution?"

"Chester suggested that Mike should rap the verses on half the album and be in the background on the other songs. Chester will sing the verses on the other half. Otherwise, this band will implode. I can feel it."

"Look, you can try him on half of the verses on the album. But if Mike doesn't cut it, you are the one responsible." David didn't look up from his computer. "You can go. Get some food. Seriously, you don't look okay."

Lying down in my office, I thought, *Mike will still be in the band, the band is not being dropped, I still have a job, and we are going to finish the album.* Ariana buzzed my office, and the ring ripped through my migraine like a razor.

"It's Rob, he says the band is so stressed and worried about getting dropped that they can't focus. He's asking for you to come to the studio at four to talk to the band."

Later that day, at NRG, their faces looked cold and uninviting as the heavy studio door sealed us in.

"Guys, I know I am not your favorite person right now, but I did just get David to agree to Mike being on half of the album."

The band shook their heads. "But hold on. We'll record Mike on as many songs as you want, whether it's verses, pre-choruses, or choruses. Whatever percentage of the album Mike is on is fine with me, and I'll deal with the blowback after we make the album. But that means I'm gonna be super critical about making every single second of this project incredible because David is looking to prove us all wrong."

"It's still an insult to us," Brad said.

"Yes, but that's the business. Look, you're the artists. You need to stand up for what you believe in. I have to stand up for what I believe in, too. We are all pissed off. Instead of complaining, take the risk and put your anger into your performance. That's what artists do."

Sticking out my hand, I was surprised when they all shook it. I had no idea where I stood with them. I was learning daily that no one could be trusted. That night I got calls from Rob McDermott and Chester guaranteeing that the band's animosity toward me would blow over. But the only guarantee in life is that there are no guarantees.

CHAPTER 45

YOUR FUNERAL

ON THE DRIVE HOME I WAS GRATEFUL FOR EVERYTHING I had in my life. My job, my family, my health, my dogs, my bands, the label, my wife. Damn it, I loved the guys in Hybrid Theory, so why was there so much drama? I would focus all my positive energy on them.

The next day I went down to the studio. focussed on A&R'ing the best album ever. First, I wanted to scrap "Pictureboard." It wasn't a strong enough. song. I knew the band would be upset, but they'd have to trust my instinct. "Papercut" was the better alternative. "Untitled" was a potential hit, but it wasn't coming out as I had hoped, either. It needed to be improved.

"Don, I just think the rap verses in 'Untitled' could be stronger. He can write better."

"You know what you're getting yourself into?" he replied.

Pushing the talk-back button, Don shook his head and whispered, "Your funeral."

I spoke to Mike through his headphones, "I'm not feeling the verse on 'Untitled.' It feels a little sterile. Back when you were making the demos, you had a unique and natural signature flow. You need to find that again. Dave Draiman of Disturbed has his signature 'wha-ah-ah-ah' vocal riff and accent; Aaron from Staind has that low, droning, identifiable voice; Chester has a unique tone; and Fred Durst has an identifiable flow."

Ripping off his headphones, Mike said, "You want me to sound like someone else? I'm not rapping like Fred." He was clearly offended.

"I want you to be immediately identifiable when someone hears your voice."

Mike held the headphones to his ear. He parodied Fred, and it sounded awful. I felt like an idiot for even making the reference. Shaking my head dramatically, I said, "I just want you to experiment with your voice, find *your* sound. Just relax and get outside your mental block. I know you got this."

I looked at Mike through the soundproof glass separating us, standing there at the mic, shoulders low, almost as if he were deliberately not giving it his all. I pushed so hard without regard to his feelings that I reached the point of no return. Something in me just kept pushing until we were both drained He wasn't defeated, he wasn't inspired, he was just done. Done listening, especially to me.

Looking back, maybe I just wasn't communicating or listening to *him*.

Mike took off the headphones. "I need a break," he said.

I had the best intentions, but I knew this wasn't the way to inspire confidence. I felt like a football coach on TV, losing his temper and yelling at a player on the field. The kind of coach who's despised and whose downfall is wished for but leads the team to number one in the league. That's all that matters. Winning. Isn't it? The only problem was I didn't have the stomach to be that type of coach.

Ross Robinson told me he had thrown things at Jonathan Davis from Korn, jumped on his back and hit him, in an effort to get him to get angry and perform better, and supposedly, it had worked. This technique clearly wasn't working with Mike. I was just bullying him, and I didn't like it.

"I can't work with you here," he finally blurted out.

"Okay, man. You got your space. But this song needs work, so I'm leaving my notes."

Leaving the studio, I was sick with my inability to communicate with Mike, who seemed to handle the immense pressure and keep his calm. But I could see something was about to break. My heart started palpitating, I dropped into the front seat of my car, looking at myself in the rearview mirror. *Get control of yourself. It's just a fucking record, with some kids from Agoura. Mellow out,* I thought to myself.

Just then, as the world was blurring, a hand banged on my window, sending me jumping out of my seat. Turning to my left I saw Chester's face.

"What the fuck? You scared the shit out of me." I rolled the window down and a cool night breeze brushed against my face like a welcome caress.

"You look like shit. You okay?" Seeing that I was unable to respond, he continued, "I think Mike's going to get it. Don't worry."

"I am worried, but thanks. I know the song's a hit."

"That's what I need to tell you. I don't even know if I'm feeling 'Plaster.' It seems so basic and not as intelligent as the other songs. And 'Crawling,' I'm just not loving it."

I sighed deeply. "I appreciate your input, but the songs you just told me you don't like...are *hits!* 'Plaster,' 'Crawling,' 'Points,' and even 'Untitled.' They're all potential hits. We just need to get them right. I'm so stressed out right now."

"You need a break. Go home and get some rest."

CHAPTER 46

GRANDMA ZEN

It was late April and I drove to Malibu to hang with my grandmother at her mobile home. We sat in her living room as she flipped through albums from Cheap Trick, AC/DC, and KISS. Holding up *Love Gun*, she said, "Remember when I bought this for you? You had no idea what the lyrics meant," she laughed. "They were all sexual innuendo. But you loved it even though you didn't understand."

"Grandma, you're a trip. You're much cooler than Mom and Dad."

"Ah our favorite," she said, pulling out Queen's *The Game*, placing it on the turntable. "You used to feel so good about music. I'm concerned. You look stressed out. You need to breathe. How did that doctor appointment go? You still having chest pain?"

"He said it was stress, that I need to relax."

"You need to maintain your creative energy and not lose control of the great joy music brings you. Listen to everyone with the best intentions, but never make decisions based on fear or trying to appease other people, because if they're wrong, then you'll never forgive yourself. But what do I know? I'm an old woman."

She hugged me, and I could feel her warm heart sending me good energy in the salty Malibu air. "You know what, Grandma, I'm gonna call the band, tell them how positive I feel and how much I appreciate them."

"That's something you do in person, not on the phone. Hang in there, kiddo."

Heading home I walked through the door as my cell rang.

"Hey, Brad, what's going on, buddy?"

"You're like one of my closest friends, and I hope you can understand, but the band just feels it's better if you aren't down in the studio so much. It's too much pressure on Mike. Please trust me."

All my grandma's good energy left my soul, and I reacted, not properly assessing the situation. "Brad, this is not how you deal with friends. But from here on out, it will be all business. End of story. You have my notes. I'll give you plenty of space, but I'll be by the studio to check that things are moving in the right direction, and the album won't be finished until we are *all* happy with it."

I hung up the phone, offended beyond belief, feeling completely unappreciated and disgusted. But then I realized that whatever I was feeling, Mike and the band were feeling it twice as hard. I looked in the mirror, and that old feeling of self-loathing came rushing back. No one could hate me the way I hated myself, and I turned it into an art form. My grandma's zen nature was completely extinguished.

CHAPTER 47

THE RADIO TEAM

I WALKED INTO NRG A FEW DAYS LATER WITHOUT WARNING. Half of the band were in the lounge, and they were quiet as I walked past them into the recording area where Don sat editing.

Smiling, Don said, "Hey, Jeff, you okay?"

"All good. I just want to hear how things are progressing. Can you play me the latest stuff?"

Listening for about twenty minutes, I felt relieved. "That one song 'Plaster,' it could be a radio hit, but something's missing. Mike's sounding much better, too. Is he around?"

Mike walked into the room with a bottle of water in his hand and a half-sincere smile on his face. He wasn't expecting me. "I was just listening to everything. It's definitely improving." He took a seat nearby. "Your performance seems more sincere. I know I can be really intense and can come off as insensitive, but I've got a lot on the line and you do, too. Sorry."

"I'm doing the best I can," Mike replied as he walked into the main room set up with a vocal mic. "Do you really need to be here?"

Through the talk-back Don told Mike, "Jeff represents the label. He's here to help."

I sat at the console, and Mike started to get a flow. I tried to say encouraging words when I felt he was in the zone, finding his own sound, but I could tell he didn't want me there. Don worked on making me a copy of the roughs for the following day.

The next day I bounced from office to office, playing the songs for executives in various departments, trying to get them invested in the music and the band.

Poking my head into Rob Goldklang's office, his cherub-like face peeked out from behind his phone. "Hey, what's up, buddy?" he said with a smile.

"Hey, man. We really don't know each other that well, but since you're in modern-rock radio, I'm hoping to get your input on this new band, Hybrid Theory."

We spoke for about ten minutes before he played the CD, listening through to almost all the songs. "This is good, really good," he said, nodding his head. "You mind if we go into Mike's office to hear it on his speakers? He may have some more insight for you."

Stepping over the clutter of Rob's office into the considerably larger office of Mike Rittberg, we played a few songs. Rittberg, tall, thin, and with a relaxed smile on his face, said, "This is good. We need radio records here, and this sounds like it's close. You should wait to play it for us, but thanks for coming in."

Just then Peter Standish, the band's product manager, poked his head in. "Jeff, can I grab you?"

"Sure, Pete." I left the CD with Rittberg and accompanied Pete down the hall.

"I know you like keeping people in the loop, which is nice, but just back off for a while. I'm doing you a favor. The vibe is that you're coming to people too soon. They know your intentions are good. Just wait until it's finished to play it for people," he said as he walked off.

A couple hours later I was looking over the NRG studio billing, extra charges, overtime. We were going over budget. Then Ariana yelled, "Rob McDermott on line four."

"Yo, Rob."

"Hey, man. Not trying to bring you down every time we talk," he laughed, "but I got a call from Standish saying you're talking about Hybrid Theory too much."

"You're kidding me."

Rob sighed. "Don't sweat it. I just told Peter, 'Who cares if Jeff talks about the band? Let him talk about it. He's passionate. Let him do his thing.' The good news is right after Standish called, I got a call from Mike Rittberg and Rob Goldklang. They're really excited, and they're the guys that really matter. Most people can't hear the details you're envisioning through the rough mixes. Just give them a record to work at radio, and they'll love you." I could envision the smile on his face, and it helped.

As soon as I hung up with Rob, Ariana yelled, "David Kahne, line three." My breathing shallowed.

"I hear you're playing music for the label execs. This isn't how we do things. I should hear the music before you play it for anyone else. I just listened to it, and the rapper's all over this."

"It's not the final cut. I'm doing my best to do what you want, what the band wants, and what I think makes the best album," I said, annoyed.

Later that evening, Ariana buzzed my phone saying Phil Q, the president of Warner, wanted to see me in his office in fifteen minutes.

"How do I look?" I asked her.

"Like shit on a stick. You look exhausted and pale."

"I may be out of a job. You don't get called into the president's office for nothing."

I entered Phil's office on the top floor shaking inside, but he appeared warm and inviting. "How are you feeling here at Warner?"

"I love it. But honestly, it's been kinda rough making this album."

"That's what I'm hearing. No one said the job is easy. But we wouldn't have hired you unless we thought you could be a strong VP. What's going on?"

"Well, I'm getting some resistance from David. He's been pushing me really hard to get rid of the rapper, Mike, and to use one of his artists, Mad Lion, which is causing friction in the studio. The band is scared they're going to get dropped, and I feel like I'm on the verge of getting fired. So, if that's what this meeting is about, please just give me a chance to finish making this album with the band. I promise it will be good if I can do it without interference."

"Relax, Blue. You don't know this, but I was one of the people who rallied to hire you. I did my due diligence, and people had nothing but good things to say. I'll talk to David about giving you and the band some space. I will give you all the room you need to run with, and the team to back you and the band. Don't be afraid of offending anyone. Not the band, David, or me. You're in charge, so don't accept anything until you personally feel it's the best it can be, okay? I've got your back."

"I appreciate that."

He pulled up a chair next to me. "You know, Quincy Jones told me how everything is cyclical, like clockwork every six years. Rock's been out of favor for a while, and it's time for a comeback. And Blue, man, we have almost no rock records here at Warner Bros. If we can shift Warner Bros. into rock with this record, I know we can't get hurt. We have no other band or album like this. I know you know rock. So make it great."

"Thanks for understanding."

Walking out of his office, I felt a huge weight had been lifted. He was the type of person I strived to be. Honest, genuine, engaging, bright—someone who made people feel good. I paused in the hallway, realizing before I spoke to him, I felt like the walls were closing in. I wasn't making the band feel good because I wasn't being made to feel good. I was determined to change that. Whatever I was going through was irrelevant. The band needed to feel good about themselves and the work they were creating.

CHAPTER 48

WAIT FOR THE BRIDGE

A COUPLE DAYS LATER, I GOT A CALL FROM DON TO COME down to the studio.

"Take a seat," he said before pressing play. "Plaster" blasted out of the speakers. When Chester's vocals soared in the chorus and Mike hit "One step closer to the edge," I lost my mind.

"This is fucking amazing!"

"Wait for the bridge."

Chester's explosive "Shut up!" bridge burst out like a breath of fresh, beautiful anger unleashed upon an unexpecting world that was about to be blindsided by a new voice.

I stood up and tears came out of my eyes. "Yes! Yes! This is a fucking statement. A command. Fricking awesome. And not one curse word. Unbelievable!"

"We built this fort for Chester to sing in. He destroyed the shit out of it," Don said with a smile.

Just then, Chester walked in. "You like it?" he asked.

"You're a monster, a beast. I love it. This song is definitely your first single."

I walked into the lounge. "Guys, this new bridge is amazing. It's like a radio-friendly version of Rage Against the Machine's 'Killing in the Name Of.' You achieved the intensity without the curse words. I'm truly amazed. We're still on for barbecue on Sunday, my new house. Let's consider it a mini-housewarming party."

It was a beautiful weekend. Chester and his wife came over to hang by the pool. Chester and I were throwing hoops in my front yard when he asked me, "What's your favorite song on the album?"

"That's easy, 'Plaster.' 'Untitled' will be a hit, and 'Crawling' is a smash," I said, dribbling the ball on the driveway.

"'Crawling.' is hard as fuck to sing. And Mike's not on it as much. I kind of feel that may be an issue."

"Are you kidding? 'Crawling' is a bona fide hit. You guys captured the beauty and the beast. I get chills every time I listen to it. Let's just hope there's no more drama."

"I can't imagine anything else," Chester laughed.

"Don't jinx us. There's always Monday morning," I winced.

CHAPTER 49

ANOTHER NAME CHANGE

ONDAY AFTERNOON, I SWUNG OPEN THE DOORS TO THE studio with yet more bad news. It seemed like we just couldn't catch a break. The band could see bad news was forthcoming by my demeanor.

"Guys, we have to change your name."

"You've got to be kidding."

"Danny Hayes called me this morning. There's a band in the Warner system called Hybrid. They're out of the UK. And there is also a label called Hybrid. Just seems like Hybrid is a diluted term so Warner wants you to change your name."

"The good news is you can name the album *Hybrid Theory*, so at least there's the relation to the name," Rob McDermott said. "The label can't prevent us from doing that."

"That's a great idea," I said. "We have an album to finish, but let's think of a new name sooner than later."

ANOTHER NAME CHANGE

After several days Brad and Mike sat me down. "We got the new name, Platinum Lotus Foundation," Mike said, spreading his hands wide like he unveiled a magical gem.

"Too many syllables. No one will remember that name. Think of something better."

"Jeff may be right," Brad said. "It sounds like PLO, Palestine Liberation Organization."

On May 1, Brad called suggesting a new name.

"Anything is better than Platinum Lotus Foundation. What is it?"

"It's Plear."

"Did you say 'Plear'?"

"Yes. What do you think?"

"Please tell me you're joking. It sounds like plastic and clear."

"Yes, exactly!"

"Platinum Lotus Foundation is better than Plear. I can't think of anything worse right now, other than maybe Crump."

"That sounds like a combination of crap and dump."

"That's exactly how your new name makes me feel. Like I want to take a crump."

"Very mature. We're serious. We've decided. So, when you send CDs please use the new name."

I called Rob immediately. "This 'Plear' name is awful. I can't approve this."

"I know. I hate it too, but the band loves it for now. Pick your battles and don't get on their bad side. They're starting to like you again."

"Are they really starting to like me again?"

"No, not really. But make some copies with the name 'Plear' and let's see how people react."

Mike called within minutes. "We also have a song by Joe that I'd like on the album. Is that okay?"

"I think that would be amazing."

On May 9, I sent out the CD with the name Plear to a number of executives. I wasn't happy with the sequence, but I showed my support and withheld my reservations.

1. Papercut
2. (Now I See) With You
3. Points of Authority
4. Plaster
5. Crawling
6. Run Away
7. The Untitled
8. By Myself
9. The Cure for Mr. Hahn's Itch
10. Pushing Me Away
11. A Place for My Head
12. Forgotten

After a couple days, I couldn't stand it anymore. I hated the name and was about to tell the band it was unacceptable, when I got a call from Rob.

"I think you got your wish," he said. "The band heard from enough people, including me, that the name sucks. They're thinking of new ones right now."

The following day we all gathered around a table outside of Warner Bros. The guys went around the table calling out new names, none of which I was liking, until Chester spoke up.

"Lincoln Park."

"What?"

"For a band name. What about Lincoln Park?" Chester said.

The table fell silent. Heads nodded slowly letting the name sink in.

"That's interesting," someone said. "Doesn't make me think of anything in particular, yet it's familiar. I think there's a huge area in Chicago called Lincoln Park. But there's also a Lincoln Park in Burbank and, I think, Santa Monica."

"That's where I came up with the idea," Chester said, enjoying the fact that we all liked his idea.

"We can make the spelling l-i-n-k-i-n," someone shouted out. "We'll never get the website domain or the dot-com with the regular spelling."

"Maybe flip around one of the letters," another said.

Rob leaned over to me saying loud enough for everyone to hear, "Marketing-wise, it will sit right next to Limp Bizkit in the CD bins. You can't get better than that."

"Oh god, no. Not another Limp Bizkit reference. That's not what we want this name for!" Mike said.

"Rob is right. It's a great thing that we are close to them because most likely listeners that like Bizkit will like us as well and they are more likely to pick the album up if they see it right in front of them. Plus they have a new album dropping soon."

Eyes rolled and heads shook at our analysis, but Rob and I knew we were right. Either way, the name was cool. It was easy to say, easy to remember, and had no more than three syllables.

"Linkin Park it is. See, when something feels right to everyone, it usually is the right decision. And you can keep the name Hybrid Theory for the album title. Now that it's settled, you can get back to the studio."

CHAPTER 50

EMPTY YELLOW PAD

TWO DAYS LATER BRAD CALLED. "WE'RE ALL STRESSED OUT, exhausted, and I'm not sure we're going in the right direction. Can you come down tonight to check it out?"

I arrived that evening to find the band looking sullen and depressed.

Don said, "Hey, buddy.. I'll cue it up for you, and you can listen in the back studio."

I walked to the back room. It was completely silent. Some scented sticks burned in the hallway. I sat by myself, took a deep breath, and cleared my mind. Pen in hand, tapping on my blank yellow legal pad, I got ready to make copious notes. Turning the volume halfway down so I could hear the details clear and balanced, I gently touched the space bar.

After going through every song for thirty-eight minutes, I realized I hadn't written anything on the pad. I listened through once more on a different set of speakers at low volume, and then once more through the large speakers cranked up high. Still no notes.

The band nailed every detail I had been concerned about. Mike's performance was engaging and exciting. The arrangements were well thought out, lean, and concise with no filler. I had butterflies and goosebumps as I walked back into the main studio where everybody was waiting. They looked prepared for bad news.

Opening the heavy door, I was unable to speak, feeling my throat tightening, tears welling in my eyes.

"Oh, god, you were in there almost two hours," Brad said. "I knew you'd hate it." Several members shook their heads.

I put up my hand because I was choked with emotion. "Guys, I have nothing to say or add other than I am so incredibly proud of you all. This is not just an album, it's a work of art."

"You're joking," Mike said. "Don't fuck with us."

"I got chills listening to it. Seriously. My legal pad is empty! No notes. Look," I said, waving the yellow pad by the binding, pages flailing about. "All we need is a great mix, but I think this album is done! And thirty-eight minutes of pure entertainment. Short and sweet! Hallelujah."

The guys all fell in. We hugged, and tears wouldn't stop coming out of my eyes. "When we all finally agree on something, we can all feel comfortable about its excellence. I am sorry for all the drama but, seriously, if all this drama hadn't happened, I don't think this album would have turned out so amazing."

No one affirmed that sentiment, but everyone was smiling and starting to unwind from the relentless tension. I embraced the happiness and walked out of the studio feeling a natural high for the first time in months.

CHAPTER 51

SHUT UP!

ORNING CAME AND SO DID A CALL FROM DON.

"I know you said you're trying to get Andy Wallace, but I'd like a shot at mixing. I know these songs better than anyone, so I won't charge you for the initial mixes."

"Hey, Don, I think we all have our hearts set on Andy. But if you're not going to charge us, I guess go for it."

On May 9, Don went in to NRG for a week to mix four songs. It's difficult for the producer of an album to mix, since a new mixer, usually brings a necessary fresh approach. Upon listening, I felt Don's mixes, while good, were a bit flat, failing to capture either the band's dynamic or the ear candy I knew they'd recorded. I proceeded to schedule Andy Wallace to mix in New York in June.

I needed to get away with my father on our traditional Memorial Day Yosemite trip. I just needed to get David's approval for the budget for Andy. As I knocked on his half-open door, he waved me in.

"Hey, David, the band and I would love it if you could come down to the Coconut Teaszer on June ninth. We're doing a label showcase to commemorate finishing the album."

"Do you have a rough you want to give me first?"

"Yup. I just wanted to say thanks for the direction and help with the album. I have a feeling this is something we can all be proud of," I said, laying Don's mixes on his desk. "We just need an incredible mix. Brad, Mike, and I are going to New York on the eighteenth to mix with Andy Wallace. I just need your signature on this budget."

"Andy's one of the best, but," he said, tapping a pen on the signature page, "Mike and Brad don't need to go watch Andy mix. That's not in their budget."

"After everything we've gone through, I'm not going to make decisions without them. And, by the way, I think Mike did an incredible job. Listen to the CD. We put him through total hell, so I'm asking you, please, for this favor. They must go."

"All right, I'll give it a listen and see if it's ready for mixing," he said. "Have a good trip."

Two hours later my office phone buzzed. "Jeff, you got DK on line one."

Shit, I thought. *That was way too quick. He either loves it or hates it.* Clenching my teeth, I picked up the phone.

"Hey, not a bad job on the album."

My mouth ajar, waiting for a 'but....' Nothing came, so I replied, "Thanks."

"You've got one song here, 'Plaster.' I think it's got a lot of promise. Let me give the mix a shot."

"I know we're over budget already, so I don't want the band to pay for any extra studio time," I said.

"No, you won't have to pay. If you end up using my mix, then pay for the studio time, but, if not, no obligation. I'll have the files sent over and have a mix for you when you're back from your vacation."

"Wow, it's an honor to have you interested. Thank you."

It was the perfect positive energy I needed as I hit the road for a ten-hour drive. David was an incredible producer and mixer, and I respected his opinion. His approval gave me the first real smile I had enjoyed in a long time.

My dad drove over to my house and embraced me as he stepped out of the car. "I'm glad we're able to take this time. These trips together mean a lot to me. We need to be thankful for every moment we have together."

"Okay, Pop. Sure. Let's get on the road. We've got a long drive with holiday traffic, and you drive like an old man," I laughed.

The second day of hiking, my dad asked me to go on an early walk. The fresh air and beautiful redwoods were invigorating. He stopped walking and looked at me just as a deer paused in the distance. It was a magical moment I would never forget. "I just want to let you know I am proud of you. I know I didn't believe in you for the longest time, pursuing this whole pipe dream about the music business. I know you've put years into this band Linkin Park. You've earned my respect. I need to tell you...," he paused just when my cell rang, interrupting him midsentence.

"What the hell, Dad, it's my boss. Sorry, hold that thought."

Hitting the accept button, I held my breath. The voice on the other end said, "I've been working on the track out here in New York over at Quad Studios, and I've got 'Plaster' sounding great. It finally sounds like a hit. Can you meet me at Scream Studios in LA on Tuesday?"

"It's Memorial Day weekend, and I'm with my dad. Is it an emergency?"

SHUT UP!

"I want you to hear this before you decide to go mix in New York with Andy. If you like the mix I can do the entire album, so the sooner the better."

I heard my Dad sigh. "I really need to speak with you, but... take care of business," he said. "Come over for dinner when you're back."

I loaded up my bags and made the ten-hour trek back to Los Angeles to meet David on the thirtieth. I drove up to Scream Studios, parking my truck in front of 11616 Ventura Boulevard. I was filled with butterflies as he led me with a smile into his studio room.

"You want a juice or a water?" he asked, while directing me to sit in his chair. "Take a listen." Tapping the space bar, the song played. My mouth dropped open as the first lyrics that blasted out over the speakers were "Shut up when I'm...!" on top of Brad's iconic riff.

This wasn't just a mix, this was major a change to the arrangement. "David, I'm confused. The intro gives away the impact of the killer bridge. Don't get me wrong, the mix sounds good, but..."

"Jeff, the song is good, but listeners won't even get to the middle of the song if they aren't grabbed right away. You need that bridge up front. That's your hook. *Now* it's a hit," he said. "Listen to it again."

"The mix is good, but, respectfully, I like the original arrangement better. Plus, it's just another slap in the face to the band."

"Just bring it to the band and let's see what they say. I think they'll realize I made it a lot stronger."

I walked out of the studio into the bright sun so frustrated, I wanted to scream "shut up!" He had me leave my father for this? I appreciated him, but he didn't understand that every time there was some semblance of peace, his good intentions created a domino effect of shit bricks.

I messengered David's mix to McDermott, who called not long after. "Dude, the band thinks Kahne's mix sucks. But let's take this as a compliment," he laughed. "For something he hated so much to begin with, he now wants credit on it."

"Honestly David's mix isn't bad; it's just another way of saying the band didn't do something the right way. It's exhausting. I definitely want to go with Andy," I said.

A few hours later I received a call from Brad and Mike. "Why are you always messing with the album? We thought we *all* agreed we were finished."

"It's not me! This is all David. I told him I didn't like the arrangement change and I didn't think you would either, but he wants your opinion. He's my boss and the head of A&R, so we have to let him do what he wants. We don't have to pay anything, and we are on our way to mix with Andy. No harm, no foul. All is good."

Midsentence, Ariana dropped a $4,000 bill for mixing and studio time for David's "Plaster" mix on my desk. "Oh shit. Guys, I gotta go," I said hanging up the phone, my mouth agape in shock.

"Ariana, please send this to Rob McDermott."

Thirty minutes later: "McDermott on line two."

"Rob, before you say anything, Kahne told me we wouldn't be paying for the mix if we didn't accept it. It's like it's intentional, nonstop drama. There's no way we're paying for it."

"I know it's not your fault, but this is bullshit. The good news is that Joe and Mike are dealing with Frank Maddox now in the art department," Rob replied.

"We won't pay for this. I promise you," I said, exhausted.

"Just make sure Mike and Brad go with you to New York."

"Done deal."

CHAPTER 52

THE TEASZER

"DID DAVID CALL BACK ABOUT THE SHOW TONIGHT AT THE Coconut Teaszer?" I asked Ariana as I was departing the office. "I really want him to see how far the band's progressed. Please follow up and make sure he knows we want him to come."

"You left David plenty of messages. Just go enjoy the show. Everyone else confirmed. I'll be there in a few hours. Relax."

I entered the venue at the corner of Crescent Heights and Sunset Boulevard. Rob McDermott, Peter Standish, and I wanted to do a show so the label could get an understanding of the band's chemistry on stage rather than just listening to the demo that was circulating.

As Rob was tuning his toms and snare, Chester was jumping two feet in the air, trying to get the blood flowing. Mike swung his arms in a hugging motion as Brad was dialing in the tone of his guitar..

Rittberg and Goldklang walked in together, followed by Phil and Julie Muncy. The band had a handful of friends arriving as well.

"Is David coming?" Phil asked.

"I hope so. I reminded him before I left."

"Another way of punishing us for not using his mix," McDermott added.

Walking up to the band, Mike asked, "Are the rest of the label coming? There's only about thirty people in the audience."

"Peter and Phil just arrived and Rittberg, Goldklang, and Grover are here. That's really who we care about. Julie Muncy and Dave Stein are here, too."

"Don't stress on that. We're gonna kill it," Mike replied.

"I love that your confidence never falters. Your refusal to feel defeated is one of the things that makes this band so resilient," I said with internal admiration.

"I've had a lot of experience in the last few months with that feeling."

Knowing that was a slight dis directed at me, I replied, "We both survived this year so far. Kick ass tonight."

I jumped off the stage and joined Phil Q and Peter.

"I'm really excited to see them. They look like they're more of a band. Even down to the way they're dressed," Peter said.

"It's so interesting. I've found that when an artist finally finds their sound, the image seems to develop naturally. They have an intensity that didn't exist before the studio."

Peter nodded to me to turn around, and the colored lights started flashing as the band walked on stage. Chester looked deadly serious, and Mike had an affable smile that turned instantly into a gritty look as Joe started scratching behind his turntables.

Chester leaned into his knee, summoning the likes of Scott Weiland, and started moving around like a snake. The band started off shaky but within two minutes their chemistry was undeniable. Chester was a natural. He was like a fish in water, and Mike commanded the stage like he was stalking prey. There was no question in my mind about the band's awesomeness. But I'd had my confidence shattered before. I was afraid to ask anyone their opinion, but right after the set, Phil and Peter pulled me aside, saying, "Blue, that was incredible. It's raw. There's a lot of promise there. The band needs some road work, but wow. The energy is electric. Much better than I imagined."

"They've been working nonstop. They had almost no time to rehearse after making the album, so I'm seriously proud of them."

We moved to the side as the band broke down their gear and another band loaded onto the stage. Mike came over to say hi to Phil, who was effusive. "Great show, Mike," he said.

"Thanks, it's been a wild ride, and we know it's just beginning. We're going to mix in a week or so. Right, Jeff?"

"That's the plan. We just need to get the approval from David," I said, nodding to Phil.

"I wish the rest of the label was here to see this," Phil added. "How's the artwork coming? The guys happier with Frank Maddocks?"

"They love Frank. They should have something soon."

Around June 15, the band came in with a logo concept—a soldier, with dragonfly wings. I stared at it for a while in awe.

"You like it?" Mike asked.

"I'm stunned. It's powerful! Seems pretty symbolic."

"It's part us soldiering on through the drama, as well as representing an army of our followers. It could signify a multitude of meanings. Frank is putting a box around our name. Looks cool, right?"

"I love the colors. Black, red, white, gray—all power colors. It has meaning, heart, and soul. Most importantly, it's reflective of the band since you created it yourselves," I said. "I'm excited to go mix. See you on Sunday at the airport!"

CHAPTER 53

DAD

O N FRIDAY, THE PHONE RANG EARLY. "JEFF, YOUR DAD'S ON line four," Ariana shouted.

"Hey, Pop, what's up?"

"I know you're busy with the album, but I really want you to come to dinner tonight." His voice sounded uneasy. "Not everything in life is work. You need to make time for family, too."

"You got it, Dad."

Heading over to his place that evening, all I could think of was mixing the album. That was the most important thing in my life. I took the elevator up to my dad's condo where he had a nice dinner set up for my sister and me. We exchanged hugs and sat at the table.

"Want a beer?'

"Nah, I'm good. How're you doing?"

"I want to go over my will. Are you okay with your new step-mom as executor? I don't want you and your sister arguing."

"Why are you bringing up a will? You're only 59," I said. I had no idea then that my dad's wife of only a few months would later push my sister and me out of our inheritance. I was only half paying attention. My mind was back on the band.

"I was having some pain, and...I didn't want to worry you until the tests came back."

My mind was no longer elsewhere. Leaning forward, I waited for what was coming next.

He paused for what seemed like an hour. "Looks like I have cancer."

"Dad, no. What type of cancer?"

My sister, speechless, ran out of the room. I could hear her crying behind the bathroom door.

"Duodenal. It's part of the intestines, the stomach."

Speechless, I walked over to him and hugged him. "I am so sorry. I don't know what to say. I love you so much."

"I'll be okay. I need to get my strength up. The good news is the doctor says I need protein, so I can eat plenty of In-N-Out," he laughed.

"I love you, but that's not funny."

I was overcome with dread. I knew he was trying to make light of it, but shit had just gotten very real.

"Let's spend more time together." I could see a tear welling in his eye, and I burst out crying. "I start chemo this week. I want to spend some time on the boat. Fridays are best, fewer people out on the ocean. And, since I bought it only a month ago, I'm still getting the hang of sailing."

"So, basically, you're saying you want to take us all down in the proverbial boat, together?" Needing an outlet, we fell into laughter. My sister, who'd reentered the room, grabbed my hand, and we held each other tight.

"Why don't you invite your friends? Invite your band. I know they'd like it."

"I don't know. There's a weird vibe."

"What do you mean? You and that nice kid, Brad?"

"Yeah, it feels like things are falling apart everywhere."

"I'm concerned about you. You work so damn hard, but I've never seen you happier than when you are talking about the band."

"That happiness has changed to stress. But let's not discuss work. Let's work on getting you healthy."

I left his condo totally confused. My life was a rollercoaster of extreme happiness and sadness. Up and down. What could I do that would be positive? I had to make the mixes the best they could be. That's the only thing in my life right now that I had any control over. Make my dad proud as quickly as I could.

CHAPTER 54

ANDY WALLACE

On June 18, 2000, Mike, Brad, and I arrived at to the Sheraton Hotel, at 811 Seventh Avenue in Manhattan, New York. On the plane ride from Los Angeles, my mind flip flopped with the pain of my father. I knew I couldn't speak to the band about what I was going through. This was *their* moment and I couldn't afford to distract them with my family issues.

It was a warm, sunny morning as we walked into Andy Wallace's magical mixing studio, gazing at the plaques on the walls, including Nirvana's *Nevermind*. The right mix makes or breaks an album, and Andy was about to pump color into the flat landscape of the NRG recordings. Every single element, every sound, can be manipulated, enhanced, decreased, heightened, brightened or darkened with EQ, drenched with effects, or simply eliminated. The three of us were on high alert. There was excitement and anticipation, but that familiar tension was back as well. At every stop on this journey, it felt like we were walking on a razor's edge and one simple mistake could spell doom.

After the introductions had been squared away and the small talk exchanged, we got down to business.

"I'll get started and let you know when there's something to listen to," the affable Wallace said with a smile.

The three of us nervously exited the room and awaited the birth of the first mix. Andy called us in after a few hours, and we pulled up chairs to hear the first two songs. I liked what he had done with "Points," but "Plaster" didn't hit me at all. I didn't sleep well that night, tossing and turning about whether I should speak my mind or wait and see how the rest of the mixes turned out. I decided to wait.

After finishing mixes on half of the songs, I headed to the Equinox to get some thinking done while working out. I put on my headphones while stepping over to the heavy bag, the Andy Wallace mixes ripping into my eardrums with fervor. My body moved in a fluid motion with the music: left jab, left jab, right hook. I could hear every detail, and as the sweat dripped off my face, my breathing intensified. I realized that this album was the perfect workout playlist, pure adrenaline.

"What kind of energy drink are you using?" a 'roided-out guy in a tank top asked.

"It's the music, not the caffeine."

"What's your favorite band to work out to?"

"Linkin Park."

"Never heard of them."

"You will."

I left the gym. I knew telling the band I wanted to tweak the mix was going to start drama, so I decided to wait and see what the remaining songs might need.

On June 23, Andy mixed "In the End," the same song that created so much tension between Mike and me in the studio. Unfortunately, it was still a problem. Playing the entire album at the Warner offices for Brad Kaplan, he agreed that "Plaster," "Crawling," and "In the End" weren't achieving their full potential. They were a little muddy and missing the detailed ear candy Joe and Mike had worked so hard on.

Andy was busy mixing the last two tracks on Tuesday, so I met with Mike for lunch and gave him my recall notes.

"We aren't tweaking the mixes," Mike said.

"We're on the same team. If you don't like the changes, then we'll discuss it after we try a recall. No harm, no foul."

Mike looked like he wanted to picture *my* face on a punching bag. He held his tongue and the expected phone call from Rob came an hour later.

"So now what's the drama?" he laughed. "Look, I already dealt with Mike. I just explained to him that the mixer is never in the groove of the record until the first three songs. I trust you. Recall the mix and the guys will have to deal with it."

Andy was the consummate professional and on board to make the mixes the best they could be. When Mike and I returned to listen, we all sat at the console. Andy seemed relaxed.

"I had to go back to the beginning, but it really has more impact."

That comment seemed to put Mike at ease, as we moved our chairs up to the console, each pretending the other wasn't there. We focused our minds, and after a few listens, there was no combat, no argument. The songs were brighter, edgier, and more defined. All the ear candy had been brought forward, the bottom hit harder, and the tops were more crisp and electrifying. Nevertheless, we both agreed something was missing.

After Andy did a third remix, we sat down at the board. Now it hit like a sledgehammer. I could see Mike from my peripheral vision, and even he was nodding his head.

"No more changes?" Andy asked, as Mike looked like he'd sear my head off if I asked for any other changes.

"I am officially one hundred percent in love with this mix," I said proudly. "No more changes."

Nodding together in agreement, it seemed like we all breathed a sigh of relief. We knew we had something special, and with the last weight removed from our shoulders, we headed home. I didn't want any days off, so I booked the mastering session for the following week. When you have something this good, you want the world to hear it right away.

CHAPTER 55

BLACK CATS, SNAKES, AND LADY FINGERS

𝕭ACK IN LA, McDERMOTT RANG WITH GOOD NEWS.

"I sent Michael Arfin at QBQ the CD last night," he said. "When I got to the office, he'd already left a voicemail saying, 'Not only do I want this band, but I have a tour for you with the band Union Underground.' He may have us starting in Saint Petersburg, Florida, on July twenty-second. It's a 98 Rock show."

"That's incredible. I know their manager, John Weakland. That could be a good tour for them!"

Everything was falling into place as we prepared for a Fourth of July party at my new house. Chester, Mike and Joe came over, and with a massive grin, started stacking a pile of sparklers, snakes, Black Cats, M-80s, lady fingers, ground spinners, and Roman candles on the large table near the pool outside for the celebration. We'd had a grueling several months, and now it was time to act like kids again. After an intense game of full-court basketball with my other band, Beautiful Creatures, Chester pulled me aside.

Handing me a beer and lighting a cigar, he said, "Man, this is crazy. We start this tour with Union Underground, we got our album coming out in February. I know this was a tough time making this album, but I want to say thanks. I know the guys wanted to kill you at some points, but they really appreciate you. By the way, I'm thinking of getting another tattoo. I've got an amazing idea of these flames for my wrists. You should get some, man. You'd look good in some ink."

"Maybe if you guys go gold. Right now, I have to focus on mastering and sequencing with Brian Gardner on July sixth. That's the soonest I could get us in there."

"Our album isn't coming out until February. What's the rush?"

"I want to be ready for anything. The one thing I've learned is that things can change in a heartbeat."

It was a bright, sunny Thursday when we walked into the platinum-flooded halls of Bernie Grundman Mastering in Hollywood. Brian Gardner greeted us in the lobby.

Everything went smoothly. Brian leaned over to me as the band was leaving. "I'm so focused on the sonics of the material when I work that I rarely pay attention to the quality of the songs, but these stand out. I think you may have some hits here. I did notice that the songs don't really have names that reflect the lyrics. Is that on purpose?"

"It's been a nagging issue for me. Thanks for bringing it up."

I called the band. "We've got all these songs with random names like 'Papercut,' 'Points of Authority,' 'Untitled,' and 'Plaster' that have no correlation to the lyrics. We need to give 'Untitled' an actual title, and our first single has to be titled something identifiable so that radio listeners will know what to request when they hear it. I think there's an obvious choice for 'Plaster.'"

"We get it. 'One Step Closer' it is."

The following day, Standish and I got on the phone with Jason Bernard at StreetWise and ordered eighty thousand samplers and one hundred thousand stickers to give to kids at concerts across the country to build awareness. An hour later, I jumped on a plane to Atlanta to see a few new bands at the Atlantis Music Conference.

It was July 14, and I was watching a rap rock band showcase at the Hard Rock with a few other A&R people. "Rap rock is so dead," a rookie East Coast A&R exec said, not knowing I had just invested my life into one such band. "If it's not *emo* I'm not into it." I winced at the comment, just as my phone buzzed.

It was Tom Biery, the always funny and energetic head of radio at Warner. "You're not going to believe this. We're at music conclave right now, and weren't planning on doing it, but we just played 'One Step Closer' and 'Points of Authority' to see what people think. Everyone lit up. It has the chance to really do something. We may want to move up the release date."

Upon returning back to Burbank a few days later, Robbie Goldklang called me to say, "We got some good early news. We sent out those black cover advances. Marty Whitney at the Edge in Arizona loves it. Mike Peer at New York's K-Rock played the song on Smash or Trash, and it performed really well. Then Mike played it for Phil Manning in Seattle, who's really digging it. Phil Q just told Kevin Weatherly at KROQ in LA about 'One Step Closer.' With the other PDs on board, he's in."

"KROQ would be massive. That's probably the most influential alt radio station in the country."

"Don't get your hopes up too quickly," Robbie replied, but it was clear that momentum was building.

CHAPTER 56

THEY'RE PLAYING OUR SONG

That Saturday, back in Hollywood Hills, I dragged the hose over to my Chevy Tahoe and filled a bucket with soap to wash the truck in the driveway. I turned on the car radio to KROQ and suffered through a car insurance commercial as the summer heat beat down. I opened the nozzle and sprayed water over the vehicle. The announcer sped through the legal mumbo jumbo and, seconds later, a song began to play. My ears perked up, my eyes turning suddenly toward the sound, as if I'd heard a ghost. A familiar riveting guitar riff blasted out of my car speakers, then an identifiable beat, and finally an intense explosion of music that sent chills up and down my spine. It was "One Step Closer"!

The hose fell from my hands and water sprayed in the air uncontrollably. I rushed to the car and opened the door to let the music out into the universe. I cranked the volume as loud as it would go. "Holy shit, holy shit! That's our song!" I screamed like a lunatic in the middle of my driveway to anyone who could hear. "Linkin Park's on fuckin KROQ!"

I raced into the house to call Brad. "Turn on KROQ! Call Mike. I'm calling Joe and Rob Bourdon." Then I called Rob McDermott. "They're playing 'One Step Closer' on KROQ!" I walked back into my driveway and jumped up and down like a little kid. The mix sounded incredible blaring through my car speakers at top volume. It was the first time I felt great in a long while.

Robbie Goldklang called a few hours later to share even better news. "The phones lit up at the station. Listeners are reacting. They want to know who sings 'the Shut Up song.' KROQ played it three times. It's incredible!"

On Monday morning, I was called into Phil's office. He stood up from his desk, motioned me in, and greeted me with a big Phil Q hug. "Ah, Blue Man. I know things got off to a rocky start at the label. But things are about to get a lot better, pal. We've got something special here." He held up an advance copy of the album. "Grover, Buolous, Rittberg, and Goldklang are our radio crew driving this project. They're playing the record for people and getting immediate feedback. I just got off the phone with Kevin Weatherly at KROQ. There's serious heat coming."

"That's amazing. I heard it on the radio this weekend!"

"It hasn't been officially added since we obviously haven't gone to radio yet, but there are like six major players who never agree on anything. But last Friday, it came back unanimous. Weatherly said, 'We don't care when you're coming with it. We're going to play this now.'"

"What did you tell him?" I was on the edge of his leather chair.

"I told him, 'Hold on, we're six months away from releasing.' He said, 'You better get it ready,'" Phil laughed. "Our hand is forced. We thought we could contain it, but these guys won't wait."

"What does that mean for our release date?"

"When these guys get excited, they know how to drive it. We're in midsummer, and we're going to have to throttle it." He inhaled deep. "It takes time to make CDs, and Linkin Park is not in the system. The plants are at full capacity pressing the big records. We have to elbow our way in and try to get enough to cover the market, because we know this is going to be a big record."

"Isn't it dangerous to release a new band during the fourth quarter?"

"We'd normally never put a developing artist this late in the year because the competition from the big artists is too fierce. But we can't wait until February. We're rushing this release because if we don't capture the momentum at radio, it's all for nothing."

"This is incredible."

"You have to appreciate that in a company as huge as Warner Bros., everything is tied to a release schedule. This move we're about to make goes against everything we know how to do, and anything the label will want to do."

I felt as if I was in the middle of a movie, the colonel leading his troops into battle with one final inspirational marching order. I rose out of the chair as if called to duty.

"What about marketing and financial support? This is too important to just throw against the wall and hope it sticks. We need a real commitment."

Phil motioned for me to sit and relax. "May and June are when the retail programs, end caps, and displays for all the hot CDs get bought by Tower, Best Buy, Target, and Walmart. I just need to move some money from Q1 back to Q4 for the band. Watch Phil Q work his magic," he said, rubbing his bands together. "The downside is costs will go up because retail placement is triple the cost compared to the other nine months."

Then, shaking his head as he looked at his computer, he said, "We've got about twenty-five marquee artists coming out with albums this fall. We're going to have to machete a path through the marketing team to make sure we have a runway to get this done!"

"What can I do on my end?"

"Get the album artwork in our hands by tomorrow or this record's not coming out."

"Mike, Joe, and Frank did incredible work, and we just need to get it approved. It's incredibly important that the band has control over the art."

"I get that the band has a couple of artists with strong opinions, but they need to respect that we know what we're doing. We need to bypass the past drama and move forward because we're up against a hard stop. We need to get to a certain place by a certain day, and we're months behind." He paused and thought some more before saying, "There's been too much nonsense already, and if someone has an issue with you or the band, they're off the project. Let's have Frank spearhead the art. Use whatever artwork the band wants."

"I know the band will appreciate that. There was a ton of drama in the office and the studio. I feel like I was too hard on the guys in the studio. I pushed my views too hard, without being sensitive to how it made them feel."

"Jeff, that's your job. We didn't hire you because you're a nice guy. It's not about being right or wrong. It's all about crossing the finish line. And if people at the label are upset with you, fuck 'em. Don't let it affect you. Once this takes off, trust me, those people who don't like the band, or don't like you, for that matter, will want to get their hooks in it." Walking over to me, he looked me dead in the eyes. "I'm not going to let people interfere with your work. If they've got an issue with something, here's the solution: I'll tell them I'll take it away from them and give the project to someone else. Damn the torpedoes, buddy. We got one, and we're going to go get it. This band will be big!"

By the time I got back to my desk, the marketing department was in full swing. Later that day I received an email with tag lines for ads: *"Linkin Park: This is the group that kicked your honor roll student's ass.""Linkin Park: Your ears will thank you." "This isn't your grandma's music."* And my favorite, *"Linkin Park: This Park ain't for pussies."*

I couldn't have been happier by this sudden turn of events. A band that was nearly shelved months prior was quickly moving to the top of people's agendas.

CHAPTER 57

TOO HARD
FOR EUROPE

IT WAS SEPTEMBER 5, AND THE LABEL WAS IN FULL-TILT LINKIN Park mode. The band was about to play a sold-out show at the Roxy, spurred by KROQ's frequent playing of "One Step Closer." The label was excited to see the young diverse crowd. I stood in the VIP area studying the audience. Usually at hard rock shows the demographic skews about 80 percent male. Tonight, the entire front row was at least 60 percent women, twenty-one to twenty-five years old. The band was hitting a different nerve with the public. This wasn't just a testosterone-juiced rock band. They had melodies and hooks that appealed to everyone.

Coming onto the stage, Brad hunched over in what would become his classic stance. Mike, with his hair dyed red, led the audience, as Chester blew away the crowd with his powerhouse voice, jumping up and down with unbridled energy.

Michael Nance from the international group leaned over to tell me he didn't understand why the head of international, wasn't getting this. "Steve says hard rock won't work in Europe."

"They're not just a hard rock band," I said.

"I know. It's basically a pop album with hard rock overtones. Every second, every guitar line, every DJ scratch, every beat, lyric, rap and melody, is a hook," Michael said.

"I'll go back. This album's way too good to *not* go international. A lot will depend on what that guy over there," he said pointing to a young guy in the crowd, "writes in *Kerrang!*"

The few days later, Nance called to tell me that "*Kerrang!* called Linkin the 'band of the moment' and said everyone should be watching them."

"That's terrific," I said.

Nance continued, "Steve is certain Linkin won't work well in Southeast Asia and Europe. I told him this album will *change* the way radio works in Southeast Asia. To underscore my point, I called the head of radio in Canada."

"And...?" I said.

"She was like, no way this will get traction in Canada. It's not for us. It's too hard rock. I told her to not think of it as a rock record but to listen for the pop hooks."

"Did that logic work?"

"She just called back and did a total one-eighty. She thinks 'In the End' could be a crossover hit!"

"That's great news. You could be that one person that breaks this band worldwide. Thank you."

The following day, I got a call from my former boss at Zomba, Richard Blackstone. "Things seem to be looking good over there," he said.

"Yup. The guys got the soundtrack to the Adam Sandler movie, *Little Nicky*. The band did really well on the road with Union

Underground, and they're coming into LA to do some media training and make their first video. The single comes out September twenty-eighth."

"That's incredible. Who's directing the video?"

"The band's DJ, Joe Hahn, wrote the treatments. We are going with Gregory Dark, a porn director. The location scout chose an abandoned subway in downtown LA."

CHAPTER 58

UPSIDE DOWN

CALL TIME FOR THE SHOOT ON SEPTEMBER 8 AND 9 IN THE subway terminal on Hill Street was 10:00 a.m., and the band was to arrive at noon. Julia Robertson, head of video, moved things along like clockwork. After parking, we were escorted into the abandoned subway, which smelled like mold. It looked as if an earthquake could level the entire underground area, but this didn't dissuade the band. Their energy was at 100 percent. Inside the tunnel, the band members prepared for the shoot. Carmen and I were with Chester and Samantha, who was anxious about Chester being hung upside down for the filming.

"I'm gonna be fine. They're fake rocks made out of foam," Chester said, pointing to the painted boulders.

"It's too dangerous. You're gonna be hanging upside down, babe. I can't," Samantha said, tears welling in her eyes. "Jeff, please stop this. He shouldn't be up there."

"He's gonna be fine, Sam. Trust us."

"You want me to trust a porn director? How does he know Chester won't fall and break his neck? I don't want my husband in any harm," Samantha said as her mascara smeared on her face. Suddenly she burst into tears.

"Babe, I need to work," Chester said gently to Samantha as he grabbed my arm and led me away. "It's gonna be okay. I'm fine, I promise."

I leaned over to my wife. "Carmen, please help calm Samantha."

"It's crazy. She's so emotional. I've never seen her this bad," Carmen said. "The band looks irritated."

"This is their first video. It's incredibly important. Just spend some time holding her hand. She'll be fine."

"You should go work. I can deal with her," Carmen said.

The video went amazingly well, and the band members were like fish in water, fully immersing themselves in the creation of their first video.

A few days later, the house phone rang at one in the morning. "Okay, okay, Sam, slow down. You want to talk to Carmen?" I asked, half asleep. I passed the phone over to the other side of the bed.

"You took a test?" Carmen said concerned.

"What's going on? Is she all right?" I sat up in bed.

"You took a pee test. Yes, of course he'll be happy! You've been married four years. That's amazing!"

"What? What's going on?"

"Samantha's pregnant!" Carmen screamed excitedly.

"Congrats, Sam!" I said. "You should tell him right away."

"I can't reach him," Samantha said, exasperated. "You think he'll be excited?

"Of course. They're probably just driving in the van right now. How's the apartment in Brentwood?"

"It's amazing. Rob Bourdon really helped out with us moving," Sam said.

"Everything is working out. Try Chester again. I'm sure you'll reach him!"

The next day I got a call from Chester. "So you heard I'm gonna be a dad!"

"Of course, buddy. That's amazing. How'd the band respond?"

"They're super happy for me. I gotta stay healthy and clean for my kid."

"I'm happy to hear that, pal. Keep your head in the game. You got a wife, family, kid, team, band, and label that are all rooting for you!"

Less than two weeks later, on the twenty-fifth, the phone rang at midnight. Sam was calling in a panic to tell us she'd lost the baby and that Chester's dad was taking her to the hospital. I called Chester to let him know how sorry we were and that we'd be there for him, whatever he needed.

CHAPTER 59

BIG DAY OUT

N SEPTEMBER 28, THE SINGLE FOR "ONE STEP CLOSER" WAS officially released. Marketing and promotion meetings went into full swing. A rollout with Noize Pollution, a street team and research company, began with them handing out promo cassettes to fans waiting in line at Limp Bizkit in-store appearances for the release of *Chocolate Starfish and the Hot Dog Flavored Water*.

Research came back and showed a mixed reaction from Bizkit fans. It showed that 5 percent of their fans in Chicago, none in Washington, DC, and only 1 percent in Maryland had heard of Linkin Park. The West Coast, however, was a different story. There, 45 percent of their fans in San Francisco had heard of the band. Even with the tepid results, 99X, a radio station in Atlanta, decided to get on board early and requested them for their annual festival.

I headed to Atlanta to catch up with the band for their appearance at the Big Day Out Festival. It was an extraordinarily hot day at Lakeview Amphitheater on October 1. I was wearing my cutoff white T-shirt and cargo shorts talking to Brad as he downed a Gatorade backstage.

"It's a good crowd out there," he said. "We're one of the first bands to go on."

"You're the newest band. It's a great crowd. It's gonna be a great show."

"We didn't get much of a line check. I hope the sound's okay."

"I'll be out there. It'll be good. Let me go say hi to Jacoby over there."

Walking over to a parked bus with crew milling around, I knocked on the door to Papa Roach's bus.

"Blue. What's up, man?" Jacoby said, embracing me. "So much has happened. Good to see you."

"You, too. Congrats on the single. 'Last Resort' is a monster."

"Dude. Congrats on Linkin. Wow, that's the same band you played me a year and a half ago? Warner did a demo deal with us when we recorded 'Last Resort,' but they ended up passing on us. We got turned down by every label."

"That's the same with Linkin, man. Forty-four auditions."

"Had you been at Warner back then, we coulda been together, but we signed with DreamWorks. Can't complain. They've been great."

"It's been a wild ride. Congrats on everything, man. I'd really appreciate it if you could check out their set. They go on in like a half hour. It would be great if you guys could all tour together sometime."

Just then, Chester walked by. "Over here," I yelled. "Chester, meet Jacoby." Chester walked over with a look like he was laser focused on the show. "Hey, I know you gotta focus, but I want you both to meet."

"Hey, man. Nice to meet you. Can't wait to see your show," Chester said with a huge smile.

"Likewise. Dude, your hair is sick. I love the color," Coby replied. "Gonna head over with Jeff and check out your set in a few."

"Thanks, man. I don't mean to rush, but I'm just headed back with the band to get ready, but I'd love to talk to you later," Chester said.

"For sure, Chester. Kill 'em out there. By the way, love the ink."

"I'm heading over to the board, but I'll meet you backstage later. This is a big show. Thanks for checking out the band!" I said to Coby.

It was already hot in the southern sun, and people were antsy. The band came out and did a quick line check. The sound guy didn't seem to care much about the band, so I leaned in.

"Is the band gonna get anything more than a line check?" I asked him.

He spoke into his walkie-talkie, which glitched and beeped. He seemed annoyed as he wiped his forehead with a bandanna. "We're running behind. Gotta get them on. Now." He spoke again into the walkie-talkie. "Three minutes."

Joe walked on stage and behind his booth, followed by the rest of the band. The audience stirred and moved forward, compacting the people in the front but leaving plenty of room in the back. Joe began with "Cure for the Itch," which transitioned into "Papercut." The crowd reaction was good, but the sound was horrible.

I was frustrated, but the crowd didn't seem to care. The energy was insane, and the pit opened wide as kids crowd-surfed over the heads of the audience. The fact that the band tore up the stage and inspired the kids despite the problematic sound was a great sign. I made my way around the crowd to Coby and Dave from Papa Roach who were stage right. I knelt down next to Coby.

"Dude, they're amazing," he said. "Chester is incredible. He's the real deal. His stage presence is insane. That crazy hair and his scrawny frame. Screaming his guts out. Where did you find him?"

"Phoenix. I'll tell you after the show," I shouted over the cheering crowd as the band transitioned into "One Step Closer." "Let's meet up in the hotel lobby for drinks round eleven."

The band finished, and the crowd went wild. I walked up to Mike, who'd just come offstage and was toweling off.

"How'd it sound?" he asked. "I couldn't hear anything on stage."

"You were amazing. The whole band kicked ass. You did great. Let's meet up in the hotel lobby after the event."

"Thanks," he said as he threw the towel over his shoulder.

It was around eleven thirty, and I was having vodka sodas with Jacoby when Chester came down. "Dude, you were incredible," Jacoby told Chester as he gave him a bro-hug.

"Thanks, you guys crushed it too," Chester responded.

Dave Buckner, Papa Roach's drummer, introduced himself to Chester and handed him a beer. The rest of the members of Papa Roach then surrounded Chester as Mike and Joe exited the elevator.

Coby greeted Mike enthusiastically. "Great show, man. I watched the entire thing. I heard you guys back in late ninety-eight."

"Oh wow. Pre-Chester!"

"Jeff played me your demos when we were trying to get a deal. We were like, 'These guys are the new kids on the block.' Our competition!"

"Hey, thanks, guys," Mike said.

"And I love your video. That shaolin ninja vibe is legit," Coby said to Joe.

Papa Roach's manager, Brett, bought me a drink. "Linkin really made an impact today."

"Absolutely. Hardest-working band I know," I said.

"The guys were thinking they should take Linkin out on the road. What do you think?"

"That would be incredible. Great pairing. Let's walk over and join the guys."

Coby leaned over to Chester, "We just got off tour with Korn on the Sick and Twisted run, and they treated us amazing. Too many bands treat the openers like shit. They gave us full access to lighting, sound, gear. It really makes a difference, and we want to do that for our opener when we headline."

Mike motioned for me to come over. "Coby just said they'd be interested in taking us out."

"Yeah, man. That's incredible news. They're great guys."

Not long after this development, I received a call from Rob McDermott about another opportunity.

"We're doing a full-court press. Arfin and I are trying to get the P.O.D. tour starting November seventh. Their management is being kind of hard-ass, though. They want a buy on."

"We're not paying to be on someone else's tour, although that would put us in the eyes and ears of a great audience for two weeks. Any other ideas of how to make this happen? When Zomba signed Limp Bizkit, to sweeten the deal we gave them a marketing fund to push the project further when the record label fund was maxed."

"That's exactly what we're doing," said Rob. "I'm discussing with Peter Standish about some marketing incentive, something that will benefit P.O.D."

CHAPTER 60

CHRISTMAS FOR HALLOWEEN

N OCTOBER 4, MY OFFICE PHONE RANG. "RITTBERG ON LINE two," Ariana called out above the clamor of demo CDs rotating in and out of my stereo.

"'One Step' is really reacting at KROQ. We just got offered a slot on the Almost Acoustic Christmas concert at the Amphitheater. They would love a song, either new or a cover, for their Kevin & Bean Christmas sampler. This is a massive opportunity. It would go a long way to solidifying our relationship with KROQ, but the band is saying it's going to be tough to record anything on the road. Can you help?"

I was able to get in touch with Mike. "Jeff, this is not going to be easy. I'd have to write and produce this on the bus. I'll do my best to get it done."

"That's all we can ask. I'm sure it will be amazing. Thanks!"

McDermott called me on the tenth to say, "The good news is, you should be receiving the song for Almost Acoustic. They recorded it in Nashville. Let me know what you think. Now, the bad news. Did you hear about a magazine that compared LP to the Backstreet Boys, saying they were put together? The guys are really upset."

"What the fuck? The band is totally legit," I said. "They all knew each other from high school and college, other than Chester. A ton of bands had help finding members. Eddie Vedder auditioned for Pearl Jam. Why are they stressing on that?"

"It's their pride," he laughed.

Just then I received a manila envelope. Inside was a CD cover printed with "My December" on it. I stuck the gold disc in my deck, just as Chester called.

"Rob, I just got the CD, and Chester's on the other line. Talk later!"

"Hey, Chester, just sticking the song in now. I can listen while you're on the phone if you want."

"I'm not sure you're going to feel it. It's a lot different than what you're probably expecting."

"Hold on," I said as I hit play. A haunting melody began. My head cocked back in wonder, as I had been expecting something upbeat. Instead, what I heard was dark and magical. My mouth dropped open and I muttered "holy shit" to myself. I'd nearly forgotten that Chester was on the phone when the song stopped. I could hear him calling my name.

"Hey, man, I'm here. I love it. I think it's my new favorite song. I'm stunned."

"Really? I didn't think you'd like it so much." His voice was lighter.

"You took Christmas and flipped it on its dark side. This is a work of art and not just a poppy little Christmas cover. Tell Mike I'm blown away."

Just then Robbie Goldklang appeared in my doorway. "What do you think? Rittberg really pushed for this."

"It's my new favorite song of theirs. Genius."

"It's good. I'm sending it over to KROQ. Let's see what Lisa Worden and Kevin think."

The next morning on the way to work, "My December" was blasting out to the public on the "world-famous KROQ." I couldn't have been happier. I arrived at the office, and Deb Bernardini sent me a promo T-shirt with the tag line, "Help Us Build Linkin Park." I took off my tee and threw the promo on just as Ariana walked in. "Mike Shinoda on line two," she said.

"Mike. I love 'My December.' Amazing job. I was just putting on your..."

"Who approved these 'Help Build Linkin Park' T-shirts?" he asked sternly.

My shirt was halfway over my head. "Well, you definitely wouldn't have wanted the other choices."

"What other choices? We should be made aware of any choices."

"We had 'This park ain't for pussies' and 'This isn't your grandma's band.' I think considering the other options, 'Help Build Linkin Park' is pretty good."

"Nothing should go out that isn't approved by us."

"This is a marketing and radio promo thing, not A&R. Things are moving so fast and people are just trying to help, but I understand your point. It should have been approved by you."

"Rob on line three."

"The band wants to toss those tees out the bus window," Rob blurted out. "The label shouldn't have made promo swag without checking with them first. I did tell the guys they can't keep being complainers. That's my job," he laughed. "They need to have some mystique."

"Either way, the promotion team is working hard. As you know, they're bundling a free Linkin promo cassette with all Limp Bizkit CDs sold on October 16, hoping that kids will listen to the free music, share the songs, and build awareness."

Warner shipped 145,000 copies of the album to retail on October 17. The official first date for in-store sales would be October 24, 2000. The label had to have a lot of confidence to ship a brand-new band in the most competitive quarter of the year.

On October 29, Phil Q and I headed out to Las Vegas to see the band perform at House of Blues with Kottonmouth Kings. It looked like it was going to be a slow night in Vegas. The crowd trickled in while we hung out with the band backstage. Phil and I surveyed the sparse crowd. "Yikes. Looks pretty empty out there."

"It's okay, Jeff. It's a new band. It's a long haul."

"I guess I was just hoping for more from Vegas."

Thirty minutes later, I peeked out from behind the stage and was stunned to be looking over a sea of young faces. The venue was packed.

"Damn, Phil, you're not going to believe this."

His eyes widened as I grabbed him by the shoulder and turned him around. All he could say was, "This is good, *very* good!"

An hour later, the band went on. Every kid in the audience was singing every word to every song, which meant that all these kids must have bought the album already and memorized the lyrics in the first week! It was an electric ocean of teenagers, hands waving in the air, moving to the beat, energized by the clamor of Mike and Chester.

After the show ended, you could still feel the buzz from the crowd. Phil and I walked out to the blackjack table. Phil threw a $500 chip down on blackjack, and a king rolled out for the first hand. My pulse raced. The second card flipped. "Bam!" he exclaimed, an ace of diamonds. Blackjack!

"We have a winner," I said.

Putting his arm around me, Phil replied, "We certainly do, Blue. We certainly do!"

CHAPTER 61

FIRST WEEK NUMBERS

THE FOLLOWING DAY, OCTOBER 30, I WAS HARD AT WORK AT NRG Studios, co-producing a new band. I made it home by three-thirty in the morning, so when the phone rang at six thirty on Halloween morning, I was groggy from exhaustion as I held it to my ear.

"Jeff, it's Peter Standish. Are you asleep?"

"I'm okay. Just a late night in the studio."

"You're going to want to wake up. You ready for the numbers?"

"Good? Bad?"

"Neither. It's great. We sold forty-five thousand albums. That's massive! Congrats!"

"That is amazing!" Jumping out of bed, I called my grandmother immediately.

"Grandma, we had a great week. The band's doing amazing."

"I never had a doubt. You love what you do. If you put that amount of passion into anything in life, you will always succeed.

But you need to take a breath and enjoy the moment. If you're always trying to outdo yourself, you'll end up losing your purpose."

"Can you come down to see the band tonight at the Palace? How are you feeling?"

"I'll be asleep before your band even goes on," she laughed. "You have a good time for me."

"Love you, Grandma."

Arriving at the sold-out show at the Palace Theater that night, I stood with Phil Q, Peter Standish, Rob Goldklang, Mike Rittberg, and Tom Biery. The band was dressed up in full Halloween makeup and put on an incredible performance.

Backstage the guys toweled off and came up to the balcony. We gathered around for a photograph. Phil Q raised a glass and made a toast. "Congrats to everyone here. We've got an amazing team, an amazing album, and we're going to take this to the top. Enjoy it!"

Phil grabbed me and the radio team and pulled us aside. "Look, this night has changed things. All those other small shows didn't show what this band is about. Tonight is everything. The label finally got to see a room in pandemonium. Let's hope this continues. We have the KROQ Calendar/Best Buy signing event in a week and a half. That will be a great indicator of where things are heading. I hope we have a good turnout and that this isn't just a 'first week' thing. I have a feeling this album has legs. This band kicked everyone's ass tonight."

The following night, Danny and I went out to celebrate. We passed by Tower Records on Sunset. The iconic landmark had a massive billboard advertising the band and the new album. We were both so proud.

"Dude, we did the publishing deal in the Pacific Ocean, when the band only had one show under their belt. Now they're on the side of Tower Records. How crazy is that?" Danny said.

I ran out into the street and stopped traffic. I asked a young kid in a black sports car to take our picture with the billboard in the background as I handed him a disposable camera.

"Sure!" he said as his friend held up the cars. "I love that 'Shut Up' song!"

Danny and I jumped in the air as the kid snapped our picture. We were on top of the world.

Right after the Halloween show, Brad asked me to lunch. His surprise guest was Dave Farrell who had just left his band Tasty Snax and was rejoining Linkin. Scott Koziol was out. Dave would now be called "Phoenix." Phoenix was one of my favorite parts of the band, so aggressive and detailed, he solidified the chemistry and intensity of Linkin Park, and a fresh new fervor on stage was about to begin. They were about to explode.

A short time later, the band, along with Goldklang, McDermott, and me, rolled into the KROQ studios, where they were doing the top five songs at 9:00 p.m. The countdown started to roll when it was announced that Linkin Park had the number one song. We all walked out feeling a monumental satisfaction that things were trending up, but we still had no idea how far it could go.

CHAPTER 62

MEXICAN PHARMACY

CHESTER WANTED A BREAK, SO, BEFORE JUMPING ON THE Kings of the Game Tour with P.O.D. that was set to begin on November 5, he, Samantha, Carmen, and I packed up my SUV and headed out for a quick trip to Rosarito Beach in Mexico. After checking into our hotel on the beach, Chester made a quick trip to a Mexican pharmacy. The wives had their bonding time as Chester and I grabbed a six-pack and walked for a bit on the warm sand, which sank beneath the weight of our feet.

"This is beautiful. This sunset is amazing, and holy crap, did we need this break," I said.

"It's just been about a year and a half since you first called me, and my life has been a whirlwind trip ever since that day. Up and down. To think I almost gave up and went home." Chester stopped and looked at me and then out at the sunset. "I don't know, sometimes I know I got it made and all my dreams are coming true, but it's like not really happening to *me*. I mean, I know I should be enjoying it."

Looking at him on the beach I saw a detached, sad look in his eyes. "Buddy, you just finished an *incredible* album, it's doing great, your voice is so meaningful, and it will touch a lot of people. What do you mean?"

"I don't know. I'm just not happy. You told me you get depressed sometimes, right?"

"I've been there, man. During the recording drama, I got real dark. I just did the best that I could." I put my hand on his shoulder. "Look at this sunset and the water. No joke, take a moment and breathe. Taste the beer, breathe in the ocean air. Look at this sun go down over the ocean. This is living. Money can't buy a sunset like this. Take it in."

"You're right. I'm fine. I just get into my head too much sometimes. Let's finish these beers and walk back. I want to make sure the girls aren't spending our money before we make it," he said jokingly, but dead serious.

That night we had fresh lobsters at an outdoor cantina, walked back toward the hotel beach, and made a small bonfire. We tossed back tequila shots with beer chasers. Taking funny pictures with our new camera, Carmen and I enjoyed the moment with our friends. The laughter rose into the night and above the stars, as we reminisced about the past year and looked forward to the future. Chester fell silent for a while, seemingly trapped in his thoughts. Within a matter of minutes, his mood swung from light to dark. He suddenly seemed to be a totally different person. As he stared into the flames, he moved his head back and yelled, "Fuck!" Then he threw his beer into the fire, sending flames up into the night sky.

Carmen and I jumped back quickly, gaining our balance in the sand. Chester stumbled forward, and I went after him so he wouldn't fall into the fire.

"Fuck it all!" he screamed in anger.

Carmen moved to comfort Samantha, who was visibly frightened. She walked her back to the hotel, leaving our camera and empty bottles in the sand. An amazing night turned inexplicably dark within seconds, without warning.

"Chester, what's going on? What the hell just happened? We were all having a blast."

"I know, man, I'm sorry. I just had too much...and...I'm sorry.... Nothing seems to be in synch, like I don't fit into any of it." Putting his arm around my shoulder, Chester said, "I'm sorry, man. I'm so fucked up."

We walked back to the rooms. Samantha joined him, consoling him, forgiving him.

The following morning, we all had breakfast, and no one spoke of the previous evening's drama, until Chester and I went to check out of the hotel.

"We can talk whenever you feel like it," I told him. "You seem like you have a ton on your shoulders."

"Sometimes I lose control. There's a lot I am dealing with, and I may have gotten some messed-up stuff at the pharmacy," he said with a sigh.

"Don't fuck with drugs, man. I don't ever do anything, and I know the guys in the band are super against it. You just need to keep everything under control. We were a little scared last night. We heard a lot of yelling. We don't want someone to get hurt."

"My past comes bubbling up as anger, sadness, I don't know. There's a lot of shit in me. And don't say anything to anyone, but I'm feeling a lot of weird vibes."

By then Samantha had joined us and chimed in, "He really loves the band but feels a little bit different from the rest of them." Chester put his arm around her and sighed.

"I'm sure they love you," I said. "It just takes time, like in any relationship."

Chester thanked me for breakfast, and, as we were walking out of the lobby, a boy about thirteen years old pointed at us and whispered to his sister, "That's him. That guy over there, with the flame tattoos."

I walked up to the kids. "I overheard you guys. What are you talking about?"

"The guy you're with. He's in a band on MTV."

"He's the singer. The band is Linkin Park. You want a photo?"

They handed their disposable camera to me. "Chester, come over here. These kids saw your video on MTV and recognized your tattoos."

"Wow, can we see your arms?" they asked, amazed by the flames.

"I just got these. You like 'em?"

Chester held out his wrists and the kids touched them. "Here, let me grab a photo of you together," I said, as Chester put his arms around his two young fans. "This is just the beginning, buddy. Watch out, world. You just got your first fan sighting in a foreign country."

Chester laughed and flashed his enormous smile, before giving me a hug. We piled into my truck and headed back home. It rained the entire way back.

As I was dropping them off at their house, Chester said, "I'll see you when we get off tour. And don't forget, we're coming over to celebrate New Year's with you and Carmen at your house."

"Wouldn't have it any other way," I said, hoping he'd be okay.

CHAPTER 63

FROM CRICKETS TO SOLD-OUT TICKETS

HE WEEK THE P.O.D. KINGS OF THE GAME TOUR STARTED, Arfin called me with great excitement in his voice.

"Last night was incredible. Kids lined up far beyond normal before doors opened. When the band went on, seven hundred kids pushed up to the front and knew every fuckin' word. It was magic. You hardly ever see that type of reaction for an opener."

"Awesome news! The band's been incredible with staying after the show, signing merch, engaging, and greeting fans," I said.

"The guys are there at the merch booth before and after the show. They're not leaving until the last fan is gone," Michael said.

"That's dedication. All these other bands are having their merch guys do everything. They're not engaging with the fans the way Linkin is."

"That's the key to building this band. Fan engagement. Every last kid."

FROM CRICKETS TO SOLD-OUT TICKETS

On November 11, 2000, I arrived at six in the morning at the Best Buy parking lot in Westminster. KROQ was sponsoring an event to promote their calendar, and Linkin was the featured attraction. It was a good way for the band to strengthen their relationship with the powerhouse radio station, to excite an important retailer, and to build their audience. I was hoping we'd get two hundred to three hundred fans to fill out the store's huge parking lot, but, at the moment, no one was there.

My friend Christian called. "I'm bringing the kids down, but there must be an accident. The traffic is stopped and exits are blocked."

Walking beyond the empty parking lot, I saw what looked like a traffic cluster. "Shit, man. LA traffic is always a mess."

Then Christian said, "Holy shit. A cop just told me this traffic is for a band performing. They're letting traffic through now."

The cars started to file into the parking lot. The KROQ vans were out in force, handing out stickers. The crowd was electric. Rob McDermott put his hand on my shoulder, and Robbie G. came over with a smile from ear to ear. "This is big. This is really big. We expected five hundred kids at most. They're saying over five thousand kids are here. They're going to sell a ton of KROQ calendars. Lisa and Kevin are super excited. Not only does it go to charity, but this is going to stoke Best Buy to make monster buys of the album."

In the midst of all this, my dad phoned with bad news. "It" was back. My dad's chemo had looked like it was working, but it rarely does. It seems every time we get over one hurdle in life, there's another mountain of worry around the corner. Life suddenly took on a deeper meaning. I was trying to look at all the positives. The band and I seemed to be getting along well, but now my father was back in chemo and fighting for his life. He was too ill to go to Acoustic Christmas.

On December 17, I left the office only a mile away from the Universal Amphitheater. We drove onto the back lot where we were escorted by two six-foot-five-inch security guards through the back entrance to the stage. I met Danny Hayes there, and we gave each other a hug. Throwing the lanyard with the Linkin Park VIP laminate around my neck, Rob Goldklang and I walked around the barrier to the front under the stage, which was partitioned off for some select lucky fans.

Linkin Park was opening the big night. They began with "My December," proving that they could go from beautiful ballad to screaming melodic rock. The crowd was immediately engaged, pushing Rob, Danny, and me up to the front. It was only two years ago that Danny and I had been at the front of the Whisky a Go Go stage and the entire audience had cleared out, leaving us with an option: either stay and continue to believe in Mike and Brad or walk. We stayed and kicked ass right along with the band. The odds of that same band being number one at KROQ and opening Acoustic Christmas was a million to one. The universe seemed to be in sync with our dreams, and tonight the electricity was palpable. I felt proud of myself for sticking with what I believed in. I deserved to feel good for once in my life. That feeling was foreign to me, and suddenly I felt overwhelmed.

Rob turned to me. "Dude, are you crying?"

Tears were streaming down my face. I wanted my father to see this. My grandmother. My mom. I didn't know what to say because I didn't know how I was feeling, so I just replied, "I'm so happy. I can't believe how amazing they are. All my dreams are coming true, but they're all falling apart." I hadn't told him about my father, how I wished he could be here to see how incredible it was. All the hard work paying off, but everything was a mess. Through the happiness and pain, I let the tears run through my confused mind.

"Watch. Next year we will be headlining this show!" Rob said.

The concert was amazing, with Deftones, Disturbed, Green Day, Incubus, No Doubt, Papa Roach, and Weezer all entertaining an enthusiastic crowd. Backstage, Goldklang and I drank a couple beers, while Lisa Worden came over and congratulated us on the exploding interest in the band. "We are one hundred percent behind these guys. Linkin Park is part of the KROQ family, easily the local favorite, and one of the most-requested bands we have on the station."

Danny Hayes took me aside in the Green Room. "Bro, people are talking about you in a good and bad way," he laughed. "When you were at Zomba, everyone was like who's Jeff Blue? Then you signed publishing deals with Macy Gray, Korn, and Bizkit, and people were like, 'That guy's got good ears. I love that guy.' Now that you've had this huge success with Linkin, the same people now talk about how much they can't wait for you to fail. People like you on the way up, but they love to watch you fall even more."

CHAPTER 64

FROM PLEAR TO PLATINUM

On TUESDAY, DECEMBER 19, I RAN INTO THE OFFICE TO WAIT for the latest SoundScan numbers. Peter Standish phoned my office. "So, you want good, better, or best news?

"Any news that isn't bad is good."

"You okay, man?"

"I'm just having some family issues."

"Well this should cheer you up. *Hybrid Theory* has been officially certified gold, but I think you know that. Better news is the plaques are on their way to your office. Should be there tomorrow."

"I can't imagine what's the best news because that's awesome news!"

"The best news is as of today we just shipped platinum!"

"This is insane. I want to surprise the guys. They are playing Sacramento. That's an easy, quick trip. Don't say a word to them!"

The next day I opened my own personal gold album. The frame was designed to look weathered and beat up. The familiar winged soldier was emblazoned on the glass sitting on top of a brilliant gold album. It was an honor to hold this beautiful commemoration in my hands after such a long and intense struggle.

Packing up the additional plaques with the guys' names on them, we carefully placed them in protective casing, and I took the massive package with me on the flight from Burbank to Sacramento. Getting to the venue early, I secretly unpacked the box and left it in the dressing room lockers backstage. The guys were taking promo pictures at the state capital in the quad under some barren trees. The eerie backdrop would end up on the band's platinum album artwork, so it was an especially ironic day. Arriving back at the talent holding area at Sacramento Memorial Auditorium, I asked the guys to assemble.

"What's up?" they asked.

"Guys, these past several years have been anything but easy. We've had great times, struggles, mistakes, and hardships. The one thing that never stopped was our determination to succeed and make history. It is such an honor to see you guys grow, and I'm blessed to be a part of it. I know we talked about someday going gold, and I wish I could tell you went gold today...."

A look of disappointment swept over their faces. "But," I continued, "in actuality you just went platinum! So, I apologize, but the plaque company can't make these plaques quick enough. Without further ado, I am proud to present Linkin Park with their first ever official *gold albums*. Platinum albums will be coming next week!"

Ripping off the brown paper wrapping, I presented each member with his own plaque signifying five hundred thousand albums sold. Everyone was thrilled, hugging each other and taking photos with disposable cameras. Any animosity or resentment from the studio drama was forgotten in that moment. The feeling of accomplishment as we held the plaques was palpable, energy emanating from our hearts with the knowledge that what we were each holding in our arms had been no more than a dream nine months earlier. It was a day to remember, and we all knew it was just the beginning of a lifetime of achievements.

That evening's show was incredible. I stood on stage watching a packed venue sing back every single word. I hid the tears of happiness that rolled down my face. I was happy for the band. I was proud of them. I admired them. The guys came off stage and smiled as they toweled off and picked up their plaques. Today was a good day.

CHAPTER 65

FROM A STEP TO A CRAWL

ECEMBER 31 ROLLED AROUND, AND CHESTER, HIS WIFE, AND Beautiful Creatures all gathered for New Year's Eve at my house in the Hollywood Hills. Everyone drank, smoked, partied, and toasted the new year.

Chester handed me a medicinal joint.

"Bro, one hit and I'm paranoid," I told him. "I don't need that. I'll stick with beer, thanks."

"The guys don't want me doing anything. It's ridiculous. We're in a rock band. We're supposed to be fucked up. That's why the saying is 'sex, drugs, and rock 'n' roll.' Didn't the band get the memo?" he laughed.

"Try to follow their lead," I said. "That's the band's culture. The guys are focused, which you have to admit definitely propelled them to success. Just be chill. We don't want another Mexico episode."

"I feel lonely on the road. I'm just not the same as the other guys. Thank god I have Samantha."

"Things will get better."

"How's your dad doing? Last time I saw him was on July Fourth? I'm not sure the guys know."

"I don't like to burden people with my problems," I told Chester. "I was more concerned about you. How's everything going?"

"Things are better. I'm blending in more with the band. It feels better overall and the" tour is going great. The tour is going great. I just want you to know the band and I really want the second single to be 'POA.' I know you're leaning toward 'Crawling,' but it kind of sends the wrong message. Not only is the song hard to sing every night, but we should have a song in which Mike is more of the lead."

"The best thing for the band is another hit. Our radio guys are the best and want what's best for you, so let's give them the credit they deserve for picking singles. Cool?"

On January 16, 2001, I joined the band to watch them perform on *Late Night with Conan O'Brien*. The band as a full unit with Phoenix was incredible. I still got goose bumps watching them, however, the ghost of the studio sessions still loomed over our relationship and it bothered me immensely.

A couple of weeks later we had the Linkin Park platinum album party in Vegas. The band was getting bigger by the minute.

Shortly after the party, I heard that Rittberg had a heated argument with the band about the single. I called Phil Q, who picked up right away. "Jeff, I know what you're calling about. The band doesn't want 'Crawling' as the second single, but I just got off with Weatherly at KROQ, and he's going to start pushing 'Crawling' no matter what. They are convinced it's a smash. But if *you're* on the fence with the band and want 'Points of Authority,' then I'm open to discussion."

"Honestly, 'POA' is one of my favorite songs on the album, and although I think 'Crawling' is a better second single, I think we owe it to the band to consider their wishes."

"Okay, I'm going to rally the troops and get them in the conference room. Be ready."

Phil addressed the tension-packed conference room. "There's been a lot of discussion about the second single. We're lucky, because arguing, healthy debate, and spirit mean people give a shit about this album. There's no right or wrong way to break an artist. So with that said, I want to hear all the reasons people have for either 'Points' or 'Crawling.'"

Twenty minutes of discussion escalated into loud arguing until the white noise was interrupted by Phil standing up and shouting, "Hey!" The voices kept debating. "Hey!" Phil yelled, slamming his hands on the table.

"This is ridiculous. I appreciate everyone has an opinion, but here are the facts. 'One Step' was big but not massive. I was hoping you would all agree on the obvious. Rittberg and Grover are behind it, and KROQ is already playing 'Crawling,' It's undeniable. The second single is 'Crawling,' that's it. We go out in April."

Shaking his head, he walked out, patting my shoulder as he walked by. "And that's the way it's done," he whispered in my ear.

"Crawling" was an instant smash, and it was soon apparent the band wouldn't question the Warner Bros. radio department again. Things were moving along well, and in April 2001, I was producing a new band at Sunset Sound and organizing the *Queen of the Damned* soundtrack. My cell never stopped ringing. Producing requires concentration, and everyone voted to have my phone silenced to prevent interruptions. I was headed home after a late night in the studio and turned my phone on to find twenty missed messages. The first five were all work related, and I started to get stressed. The sixth was my dad.

"Grandma just had a heart attack. Call me right back."

The next message stated they were headed to Kaiser Hospital. The next ten messages were the same until the last message. "I don't know where you are, but she passed." It was 1:30 a.m. when I called my dad.

"I can't believe she's gone," he said. "I don't know how long I have left either."

My grandmother always believed in me. I was sickened that I wasn't able to be there for her when she passed, but I was blessed that I could thank her for supporting me just a few days prior. The band I was working with didn't care. No one cared except my family, and I wasn't there to support them.

CHAPTER 66

LUNCH AT SHUN LEE

T HE BAND WENT ON TOUR IN EUROPE ALL THROUGH MARCH, supporting the Deftones, and returned a more intelligent and sophisticated group.

"These guys learned a lot from the Deftones," Michael Nance told me from the road. "This was an important leg." Carmen and I caught up with them in London, and I was blown away by their performance at Brixton Academy with Lostprophets. I was impressed that Chester pulled out an acoustic guitar and played a song he had written, "Morning After," as well as my favorite song from their Mudrock EP, the Beastie Boys–style "High Voltage."

I traveled to Sacramento for Ozzfest to see both of my bands, Linkin Park and Beautiful Creatures. Creatures was more classic rock, and they lived the sex, drugs, and rock 'n' roll lifestyle. As I took Razor scooters around the massive fairgrounds, watching Green Day and Ozzy Osbourne perform, I bounced over to the Creatures bus, surprised to see Chester with DJ Ashba, drinking and with a bevy of topless women around. DJ was just finishing signing some breasts, when I said to Chester, "I think the guys are looking for you. Don't let them see you this way, buddy."

"I'm good. They gotta let me be me, man."

"I feel you. I know Coby was asking where you're at. You guys are a pair, pushing the limits."

Later that evening, Brett Bair called me. "We got a flyaway for Papa Roach, Disturbed, and Linkin. Your band's blowing up, man."

Two days later Chester called me. "Jeff, it's incredible. We had a private 747. It was like a dream. We were all saying ten years ago, it was Bon Jovi and Pantera on a private jet. Now it's Linkin and Papa Roach. We are on top of the world!"

"I'm happy for you guys. You all deserve it."

When I returned home after traveling to see a few bands, Carmen told me she wanted a separation. Understandably tired of the late nights, the travel, and the stress, she had been planning this for at least a couple months. I went back to the office miserable but determined to focus all my energy on work. Chester and Samantha had warned me that even though Carmen worked and was happy, she was tired of living the life of a music executive's wife. It occurred to me that I loved my job more than anything, except my two yellow Labradors, Dr. Chubbs and Mojo.

I was now consumed with other projects I'd brought in to the label. My primary job of making the album and getting the label excited about Linkin Park was complete, and it was just maintenance and administration until the next album cycle. A couple months later, Mike called me while I was traveling.

"We are hearing 'In the End' is the next single. Jeff, we want 'POA.' There's no way we can go to pop radio on this band, and definitely no way we are doing *TRL* on MTV. That will ruin our credibility."

"Hey, Mike. First of all, congrats on how amazing everything is going. Secondly, I love 'Points,' as you know, but the radio department has done pretty well by you guys. I'd trust them. We are all working toward the same goal, and I think they're leaning toward 'In the End.'"

"We have to remain a rock band and focus on our core audience. Promise me you'll have our back on this."

I called Phil Q, who told me he was currently on the phone with McDermott. "We both know what you're calling about. It's the same story. 'In the End' is getting played. It's happening. New York, Z-100 wants an interview, and *TRL* wants 'In the End.'"

"Well, the band wants—"

"You can't worry about what the band wants at radio. It's your job to make the band stars, not be their friend. They're talented, but they don't know everything. Every band thinks they're Christopher Columbus. That's okay because they *have* to have that feeling. If you don't believe in your head you're going to be the next big thing, the lift is too heavy. They got the star power, but they don't know radio like our radio guys do, and they're saying 'In the End.'"

Rob chimed in, "Jeff, I have your back. I won't let you get thrown under the bus on this one, but remember I have to be on their side. We're going to set up a meeting with everyone at Shun Lee. It's a great Chinese restaurant in New York. We'll all be in town, and we can sit with the band and let them think it's their idea to have 'In the End' as the next single."

"How are you going to accomplish that? Hypnosis? Good luck," I laughed.

A few days later we all entered the restaurant at 43 West Sixty-Fifth Street, congregating at a huge table in the back. After the orders were placed, everyone congratulated each other for the immense success the label and the band were having. No one brought up the elephant in the room.

Mike, clearly the leader, finally spoke, "I know we are here to discuss the next single, so first of all, we appreciate everything the label is doing. Everyone has been incredible with the support. But we are a rock band, and we'd like 'Points' to be our next single."

Phil pursed his lips and prepared to speak, but Mike continued. "Press are already saying we're the 'put together' Backstreet Boys of nu-metal. The minute we go to *TRL* or pop radio, our credibility is totally lost. Even Jeff said he agrees with me," Mike said. "Right, Jeff?"

Nodding my head, I said, "Yes, I agree. We need to keep the band's cred. The problem is we have too many hit songs, and we don't know which one to pick next. This is a problem other bands *wish* they had. Let's put this in perspective."

"You know what I mean. We had this discussion," Mike replied.

Phil continued, "As Jeff says, it's a problem, but a good one. It means we're doing our job. It seems we are at a standstill once again, but this time the situation is a bit out of our control. The decision is being made for us. 'In the End' is showing up on pop stations because program directors in Dallas, Cleveland, Pittsburg, Buffalo, St. Louis, Kansas City, and others are playing it at night, and then the morning PDs come in, hear it, and it started to open up into daytime. Pop stations are playing it at two in the morning. We are about five million albums deep, so I have to put my foot down and have you do one interview with Z100."

Rob McDermott finally interjected, "Look, we get it, but we need to be careful. I don't want to be another Alanis Morrissette, where the band becomes overexposed at pop so deep that their second record stiffs. Remember, we're a rock band."

The band looked irritated and ready for this discussion. Mike shook his head. "Why even call this meeting if you knew what you were going to do beforehand?"

This was my chance to support the band. I agreed with them, but I also understood the label side. If radio was going to start playing "In the End" no matter what, then we had no choice. We were all on the same side. No one was trying to screw anyone over.

Finally, Phil stepped up. "Sorry, guys, I understand your point, but you're going to have to trust that the label has your back. We'll hold off pop radio as long as possible with only the one Z-100 interview, but we aren't going to step in front of what looks like an incredible run. You've got an awesome tour this summer. Focus on that."

No one touched the delicious food sitting on the table. The band was clearly upset. A year ago, we couldn't get a label to give us a dime, let alone pay for a classy meal and throw radio support at us. But here we were, top of the world, and the tension was the same.

After the band left, Rob, Phil, and I remained at the table. Phil said, "You'd think they'd trust us. 'In the End' is the right choice, and we're going with it."

As great as the label performed, the band performed even better. With every show they got stronger, more skilled, and more intelligent. They honed their business acumen as well, understanding the best way to monetize their careers. Word spread about the connection they had on stage with the audience. I was amazed at how they progressed on their own, so quickly and seamlessly. The band was putting the final touches on their documentary *Frat Party at the Pankake Festival*, to be released in November.

I traveled to New York to be with the band for the MTV Music Awards. Chester and Samantha were in the hotel room near mine. Tensions were high, and Chester began drinking and using again. It was pandemonium the following day, as I maneuvered backstage with Linkin Park and Macy Gray. Macy was wearing a sequined dress that was embroidered with the words "My New Album Drops Sept. 18 2001. Buy It!" The guys knew they had to destroy the stage during their performance.

Dale Earnhardt Jr. introduced the band, and the guys delivered a blistering performance that left no doubt that the band was taking over the rock world. Fred Durst stopped me in the hotel lobby after the show.

"Bro, congrats," he said. "You bugged me about this band for three years. You were one hundred percent right. I should have listened." Coming from a performer as intelligent as I believed Fred was, I took the compliment to heart.

I felt good for a moment.

Then September 11, 2001, happened. The world stopped in the wake of unspeakable terror, less than a week after we left New York. Almost every American band cancelled their European tours, but Rob and Linkin thought it was important to keep playing for the fans. I caught up with them on the Family Values Tour in Philadelphia on October 22. Chester was not doing well. He was drinking and told me he was going through "some drama" with Samantha. I was hurting about my failed marriage. It was a dark time for everyone.

By the time of the Projekt Revolution Tour, there was no question how important they had become. Linkin Park came at the end of rap rock and nu-metal cycle, yet became the biggest band of the genre. With their popularity, the band wanted more autonomy, and my role became more administrative than creative. The incredible Warner Bros. machine had been working at 100 percent function, maximizing all opportunities, and the band delivered its talents that surpassed everyone's expectations.

Even with all the excitement, word came down that another regime change was imminent. It seemed like every year things were being shaken up, and it was clear things were about to change again.

I was approving budgets for the *Reanimation* remixes, and could tell things were a bit distant with the band. Then, one afternoon at Sunset Sound, Rob McDermott dropped by unexpectedly to deliver a message.

"This is a hard thing to say, so I'm just gonna say it. The band doesn't want you involved anymore."

"What do you mean?" I asked him.

"All the shit that went down in the studio took a toll. I told the guys, 'Let it go. Jeff's great at what he does.' But they're huge now, and they can't let it go. You're still involved from an admin perspective, but, creatively, they are in charge. Period. You and I will always keep talking, but let's let this rest for now. Keep it friendly. Give it some time."

I felt nauseous. "Just like that? After all I did for them? I gave everything I had, put everything on the line. I know I was really hard on Mike, and things got ugly, but look at how it all turned out. Can't we at least talk? I mean, why are *you* telling me this?"

"They sent me here because they don't want to talk about it. A lot of politics and fucked up stuff happened, but this is what the band wants. I'm sorry."

My head was swimming. My legs felt like they had been swept out from under me. My heart was being ripped apart at the seams. Now I knew how Mark and Mike felt. And it sucked.

CHAPTER 67

IT TAKES A VILLAGE

F EBRUARY 2002 WAS AN INTENSE MONTH. AT THE 44TH Grammy Awards, Linkin Park was nominated for Best New Artist, Best Rock Album, and Best Hard Rock Performance for "Crawling," which they won. Despite what every label called "nothing new" back in 1999, the band won a Grammy with their new genre of music combining hard rock, pop, metal, rap, and hip hop with amazing melodies.

That same month, my divorce became final, and in March, my maternal grandmother was on her deathbed at West Hills hospital. I had missed the final moments with my paternal grandmother and was determined not to let that happen again. I stopped by the supermarket to pick up flowers for her, and at the checkout, there was the new March issue of *Rolling Stone* with Linkin Park on the cover. I was thrilled for the guys, grabbed a copy, and brought it to the hospital to read to my grandmother.

When I kissed my grandmother's head, she was barely coherent. I opened to the two-page spread and began reading. One of the first names mentioned was mine. Instead of joy, dread came over me. I was honored to have been in the article and an integral part of the story, but the piece focused on Chester. I knew there would be some fallout with the rest of the band.

I stayed with my grandmother a while, distracted by the article. On the drive back to the office, I called Rob and asked him whether he'd read the *Rolling Stone* feature.

"The band wasn't too happy that your name was mentioned before theirs, and it was more an interview with Chester," he said. "But he gives the true story, and he credits you with discovering him. It will all blow over."

"It's really a testament to the label that this band is blowing up like this," I replied. I realized that Warner Bros. was a true village, everyone coming together to break Linkin Park. "We really couldn't have done any of this without everyone jumping in at the right moment when they realized what an incredible album the band created. Fran Alaberte, Dave Stein, Yvette Ziraldo, Amy Zaret, Phil Q, Jessica Bardas, Peter Standish, Tom "Grover" Biery, Wagner, Mike Rittberg, Michael Nance, Kevin Sakoda, John Boulos, Goldklang, Jody Raphael, Naveen Jain, Ariana, Julie Muncy, Orlando Puerta, Frank Maddocks, Susan Leon, Rich Fitzgerald, Deb Bernadini, Steve Margo, Debbie Pisaro, Andreas Wettstein, so many people... the list goes on. We could never have done it without them."

"There's more to come. Don't worry, Jeff," Rob said, not sounding confident at all.

Over the next several months, between the band being on tour, my work with other artists, and our tortured studio past, the relationship with Linkin, and their need for me, dissipated.

I called my old friend Lee. "I need some advice. You've known me since we were three years old. You met Brad the first week I met him, you've played poker with the guys, hung with Brad at my bachelor party, wedding, and been to all the shows and parties.

Over the last year, our relationship has been on the rocks. Despite how much I've tried, we're not close. I feel like it's the end of a bad marriage. I can't go through another divorce. It's too painful. I love these guys."

"You did your job. You were in charge of their future. Brad was like your younger brother for a while. You had a huge responsibility that relied on your ability to connect and communicate with them. You were the only one in charge for many years, and now, from what I've seen, all these other cooks are entering the kitchen. The label, your new and old bosses, managers, agents, the politics, and newly found friends—everyone stands to profit, and egos get involved. I mean, you told me you pushed Mike so hard that you felt horrible about it. Of course, they're going to resent you no matter what. Plain and simple, drama enters, and that awesome bond you had was bound to break."

"It's making me sick to my stomach."

"A married couple is hard to keep together, let alone a relationship with a band. There's too many egos involved."

"I just wish everything was back to the great feeling we had when we found out we were all going to Warner, excited to make the album, great people around us, and new energy. All of that's changed, and it's dark as hell. Looking back, I would have dealt with things so differently."

"Don't beat yourself up. You did what you thought was best and look how great things turned out for them. At least you didn't lose your wife too."

"Yeah, I did."

"Oh, scratch that. Either way, I am incredibly happy for you and the guys."

CHAPTER 68

ALONE

Y DAD CALLED AFTER HE READ THE ARTICLE AND RE-minded me that success, money, and notoriety do not bring happiness. The truth is, I was still obsessed with proving to my father he had made a great choice in adopting me.

Chester called. "Samantha just heard about your grandmother. Why didn't you tell me? I'm here for you."

"My father is worse now too. I'm going through a ton."

"We love you, man. We were just with Andy Gould, and he said, 'Every platinum artist has a dozen fathers, but every flop is a bastard.' You were the only one really there in the beginning. There's just so many people around right now."

"I appreciate the call, Chester. Things tend to get distorted. There's a whole new regime coming into the label. Lots of changes."

"No, man, you did something really special. We won't forget it, no matter who comes into our lives."

In May, Phil Q called. "It's official, Blue, I've got some news. I'm going to be exiting Warner at the end of the month. It's been an incredible ride, and I'm sure you'll be fine here without me. We had an amazing run together."

"Phil, you were the glue that held this ship together. Now I'm really concerned."

Phil Q exited, and my contract was coming up. I had offers from Clive Davis, and David Geffen among others. The new CEO of Warner Bros. graciously offered me own imprint and a new three-year deal. I was grateful. But the emotional rollercoaster had literally ripped part of my soul away from me. I figured I would stay at Warner for another three years and rekindle my relationship with the band, if it was salvagable.

The next day I received a call from my manager. "Jimmy Iovine wants to meet with you at his house in Holmby Hills. You can't pass up this meeting."

Upon entering the beautiful, sprawling estate, we discussed A&R development and the process behind Linkin Park. Jimmy was an icon who had produced some of my favorite albums and I was in awe. I explained to him that I came to realize that when it comes time to make the second album, the template had already been set. *Hybrid Theory* was such an incredible success that the chemistry and sound shouldn't be messed with. The band did not need traditional A&R guidance in the way I had done on their first album. The band didn't want me involved and felt they could do it on their own. The meeting went well, and halfway home, driving along Sunset Boulevard, my cell rang.

"You must have made an impression. Interscope is offering basically double. It's an incredible deal that Warner just can't come close to. It's your decision. It will ruin your relationship with Warner, but you can't pass this offer up."

"Oh my god. I can't wait to tell my father."

I whipped my car around and headed to my dad's place in Marina. When I arrived at his condo, he didn't look so great. I wanted to tell him how much money I was offered, but it seemed irrelevant. He was thin as a rail, and we sat in his living room for no more than a few minutes before he began to cough up blood. Then he started convulsing. It was the most horrific thing I had ever seen. I called 911 and an ambulance rushed him to the hospital. The following day, as he was recuperating, we sat together and I told him the news.

"Money means nothing," he said. "The imprint means nothing. You need to be around people who inspire you and make you happy. I never really told you enough how proud I am of you, but that environment is toxic. Take it from someone who has no time left. Every day counts. You need to do everything in your life while you're healthy." Just then, he winced in pain.

The nurse arrived with more morphine, and I held his head, rubbing his pressure points, I worked on visualization with him. I whispered in his ear, "You're on a boat. The water is sparkling, clean. You breathe in deep as the fresh air fills your lungs. The boat is lapping on the waves. Listen to the gentle sound. Close your eyes, feel the motion of the boat. Breathe."

My father drifted off. I sat watching him as my phone rang. It was Jimmy Iovine.

"How's it going? I've got one seat left on the jet with Dr. Dre, Gwen, and Bono. We would love for you to come to the Super Bowl with us."

"Oh, man. Thank you so much for the offer. I'm with my dad in the hospital. I don't know how long he has."

"No worries. I'll hold a seat for you."

When my father woke, I told him about the Super Bowl.

"Jeff, go. You have to go! Are you crazy? You need to bond with your new boss. The Super Bowl is a once-in-a-lifetime opportunity."

"No, Dad, we are going to watch it together in the hospital."

I chose to stay with my father and watch the Super Bowl by his bedside while he slept. Sixty-one years old. Too young. Nothing else mattered.

A few nights later, I decided to stay overnight in the hospital with my father. He was in a coma, and I sat by his side. His breathing for weeks had been extremely labored. The death rattle in his lungs, the smell on his breath of impending doom, and the fluorescent hospital lights were a constant reminder that nothing was permanent.

It was after visiting hours, and the nurse brought me a blanket. *The Tonight Show with Jay Leno* was on the TV above us, trying to deliver some good energy into the room. Around 11:20 the death rattle subsided. I stood up and turned off the TV. My father's breathing slowed. He relaxed. A smile appeared on my face. I kissed his forehead. His breathing relaxed even more.

"I love you, Dad. Breathe." I rubbed his earlobes, trying to use pressure points on him to relax him further, and he seemed to calm even more. Whatever I was doing was working. A tear of happiness ran down my face. "You're going to be okay, Dad," I whispered into his ear.

"Nurse, please come," I buzzed. "My father is getting better!"

I continued to rub his earlobes, and he responded by relaxing even more. His breath slowed to a normal pace. Three minutes later, it slowed even more. Something was wrong. It was too slow. *Oh no. Please no. No.* It slowed unnaturally. The breathing was way too slow, almost nonexistent. It was almost gone. *God, no.* My hope turned to fear, and I could barely breathe myself. "No, Dad, wait. I love you so much. Thank you for taking me in as your son. I love you so much."

His breathing stopped. I was alone.

CHAPTER 69

IN THE END

EMPTY AND EXHAUSTED, I WALKED OUT OF THE HOSPITAL into the quiet Santa Monica night. I made my way towards my car, parked on a nearby residential street and stood in shock. Minutes passed. A sprinkler watered someone's lawn and the mist of the spray was hitting my leg. I didn't move. My head swam. I just lost my father. I lost my band. And I was losing my sanity. I wanted to call someone but it was too late at night. What was my father's legacy? Was I it? What was my legacy? My mind jumped back to one of the last times I saw the band perform live.

My manila envelope at will call had two lanyards and two all-access passes. Breathing in deeply, I draped one of the lanyards around my neck and placed the spare in my pocket.

Moving to the underground area, I walked the long stretch, flashed my badge, and was escorted to the green room. Chester smiled and gave me a hug. The rest of the band smiled and nodded. On the surface it appeared like everything was good, but I knew there was a huge distance between the band and me, an unspoken divorce, and it hurt. We were all escorted up the stairs to where the guys waited for the entrance music.

Standing on the side of the stage, I could see the audience in the front stirring up in anticipation. The band walked out onto the stage, and the crowd erupted. Feeling a rush of pride, and at the same time a drain of disappointment in how far our relationship had fallen, I stood, arms crossed, emotionally detached, just feeling lost. I was saddened by the loss of all whom I had trusted and loved. It wasn't about the money, as my father said. It was about happiness and being in the moment.

The familiar dejected voice in my head appeared. It told me to get out of my high-end problems and self-pity. You're alive. You're healthy. The band is doing well. Hell, you've got other offers! Life has been and will always be an emotional roller coaster with dreams both fulfilled and lost. The important thing is being prepared to take the next step, whatever that may be.

Looking out into the crowd, the kids were lost in the incredible music and energy. Then, out of nowhere, someone tapped me on the back. "You work with this band?" It was the security guard who had escorted me down to the backstage area.

"I'm their A&R guy."

"This band has changed my life," he said, pointing to the guys playing their hearts out on stage. "Honestly, they saved my life. I was at my end with my wife and kids. Listening to this album really pulled me through. Thank you."

"No, man. It's the band, not me, but thank you. That means a lot to me." Before I could say anything else, he patted me on the shoulder and went rushing after a kid who was trying to jump the barrier to stage dive.

This band changed my life, his voice echoed in my head.

IN THE END

I turned back to watch the band. Mike was on fire, Chester was explosive, and the band was superior to almost anything else out there.

"You believed in this, and you were right, Jeff." I heard the words of my grandma and my father in my head. *Why do I feel like shit, then?*

I watched the audience start to push each other, everyone having fun. Walking down the ramp I came to the front of the pit where kids slammed up against the barriers. I flashed my all-access pass, and the guards made room for me.

"Points of Authority" started, and the crowd went wild, the sea of kids moving like a massive wave. I felt the rush, the emotion, the fire. I was irritated at first, then I looked at the kids slammed up on the metal rails, separating the band from the fans. They looked like they were in pain. I took another look. It wasn't pain; it was exhilaration, excitement, and enlightenment. They weren't wincing; they were smiling like this was the best night of their lives.

Turning around, all I could see was faces, all smiling, sweating, pumped with adrenaline, and passion. I focused on one person in particular whose smile stood out. She was a twenty-something, holding someone's hand, screaming every word to every song, as she kept looking down. Her dirty-blonde hair pulled back in a ponytail, she was talking to someone and laughing with excitement. The crowd parted for a brief moment, and I saw the hand belonged to a young boy, about twelve years old. Most likely, he was her younger brother. Baggy pants, checkered Vans, and brown shoulder-length hair. She was protecting him from the crowd, and he had on earphones, just like Brad's! My heart leapt as I caught his eye. He was mesmerized, engulfed by emotion, and I could instantly tell that this moment, right here, right now, was going to last him a lifetime. It was emblazoned in his memory. And now it was permanently etched in mine.

I reached out my hand and waved at them. They turned and looked me in the eyes. I nodded, and the kid smiled. Taking off the all-access pass that hung around my neck, I handed it to the young boy.

His sister grabbed it. Her eyes grew large and pointed to herself and her brother as if to say, "For us?"

I nodded and smiled and mouthed the word, "Enjoy!"

"Oh my god. I don't know what to say! Thank you!" she screamed over the energized crowd.

I winked and smiled as she placed the lanyard over her brother's neck as he looked down at it and his sister whispered into his ear. His face lit up. "That will get you into anywhere you want," I shouted. Smiling, I looked into the sea of kids jumping in the air, and within moments, the crowd pushed open, throwing my back against the barrier. A mosh pit was forming. My first inclination was to back the hell out of there, fearful of getting smacked in the head. The young girl grabbed her brother and moved to the side, and I motioned them to the backstage area.

When was the last time you were in a mosh pit? I thought to myself. Shaking my head, I knew it was years. The circle widened and sucked me into the pit like a vacuum. Bracing my hands in front of me, I was slammed from the back with a thrust, flying into a sweaty six-foot plus kid in front of me, who then propelled me into the middle of the pit like a whipsaw. Everything was out of control as I let my body freefall to the music. Chester's voice soared as Mike rapped. Just then a leg came from above, and a converse sneaker came flying into my face. *Why am I always being hit by a Converse hi-top?* The body surfer was being passed around and finally thrown back behind the crowd. The smell of rock 'n' roll energy was in full force as my nose smacked in pain from the sneaker. I felt blood. I felt alive. I was lost in the moment.

IN THE END

An ambulance rushed by, and I woke from my reverie. I hadn't allowed myself to be out of control like that in a long time. It was at that second, standing on the sidewalk at 2 in the morning, that I realized what I was on this planet to do. My purpose. Make people smile. Make memories. Let people lose themselves, provide a release from their daily angst, troubles, and fears of daily life. My purpose wasn't to make money, nor to build and feed my ego. When we go, we go. No one knows for sure what comes after, but while we're on earth, we are blessed if we can play a part in uniting people. Music has the power to unite. And we are all part of the music.

At that moment, I finally felt peace.

EPILOGUE

I**T WAS THE MORNING OF JULY 20, 2017. I WAS POURING MY** third cup of coffee, shaking off the effects of pulling another all-nighter in the studio, when Rob McDermott called.

"So horrible about Chester."

"Hey buddy, it's been a minute. Wait. What do you mean? What happened to Chester?"

"He's gone. They're saying it's a suicide."

"What? Chester's dead?" My jaw dropped to the floor, and the bitter taste of the coffee hung on my lips.

The calls started coming. Next thing I knew I was live on air with KROQ reminiscing about the first time I spoke to Chester on the phone. His loss was immediately felt around the world. Shortly after, I was on with Rob McDermott again, when my phone beeped.

The caller ID said it was Melinda Newman at *Billboard*. "Rob, let me call you right back."

I clicked over. "Jeff, I am so sorry. I know how much Chester meant to you. It's such a tragedy. Are you okay?"

"I'm just stunned. I literally had a dream about him last night."

"I don't know if it's too early, but we'd love to ask you a few questions. You were the one who discovered him back in ninety-nine and convinced him to join the band."

"You know what, this is all so fresh," I interrupted. "I haven't had a moment to process anything. I'm not really in the mindset to answer any questions."

"Well, take your time. Maybe you can write a brief piece on Chester if you're up to it?"

The phone hung in my hand as I stared out the window at my back yard, overlooking the Warner Bros. lot, the backyard where Chester and I spoke of our dreams, the future, and about doing something meaningful with our lives. The July light hit my eyes as I stood there, sunblind, trying to process the terrible news. I asked myself how someone who apparently had it all could lose all hope. But deep down I understood. Chester and I both suffered from depression. We both felt like outsiders, but somehow I thought we had made it through the darkness that he sang about so eloquently in all his songs.

My first conversation with Chester had been seventeen years earlier, in March 1999. I was drunk in a hotel room in Austin while he was drunk celebrating his birthday a thousand miles away in Phoenix, Arizona. Neither one of us knew it then, but that phone call not only changed both our lives, it also changed the world. I was able to convince him to come to LA, and Linkin Park as the world knew it was soon formed.

Memories of our trips, dinners, and the struggle to not only get a record deal, but to stay alive at the label came flooding back. Living at the Hollywood intersection where fantasy and delusion collide with reality, we're all married to the entertainment industry. And she can be a bitch, taking an intense psychological toll on all who play in her alluring web of fame. She exalts and destroys, pushes and pulls, for better and for worse, and she can suck the soul from us all. After so many years in the business, my soul felt empty. Maybe his did too.

At Chester's funeral, the July heat burned down on his friends, family, and a mix of industry types, all dressed in black. As I looked around, I wondered if any of us were really happy. How many of us would or could touch the lives of millions like Chester did? And how many of us deluded ourselves into thinking we made a difference by being associated with him, instead of actually reaching our full potential?

A music exec pulled me aside. "I read your article in *Billboard*. It was moving. Don't forget all the good times you had with him. The band helped millions of people find a reason to live." That was all the inspiration I needed. When I got home, I found a huge portion of my life tucked away in the dusty corners of my garage. Massive cardboard boxes filled with exhaustive journals, faxes, emails, notes, cassettes, DATs, and CDs, from 1995 to 2003. Boxes of material I somehow knew would be relevant, something special to be saved twenty-plus years after the fact, but hidden because they reminded me too much of the heartache that I went through during the creation of *Hybrid Theory*.

Once I opened the boxes, I experienced a myriad of emotions and memories. It wasn't just the pain that came flooding back, but the joy as well.

Rest in peace, Chester.

ACKNOWLEDGMENTS

THIS BOOK WAS VERY DIFFICULT TO WRITE. IT WAS EMOTIONALly and physically exhausting. I have a lot of people to thank. Chester and Samantha Bennington; Lee Lubin for over fifty years of friendship; my interns from UCLA, Zack Borenstein and Mason Tiratira, Ariana McClinton, Ariana Murray, Rob McDermott, Danny Hayes, Scott Harrington, Rob Goldklang, Macy Gray, Darryl Swan, Phil Quartararo, Michael Nance, Michael Tedesco, Richard Blackstone, Neil Portnow, Joe McEwen, Jacob Bunton, Jason Elgin, Jacoby Dick, Alex Berger, Michael Arfin, Adrian Miller, DJ Lethal, Scott Koziol, Chastity Ashley, Carmen Gonzales, my mom for making me get straight A's in order to get a drum set, my dogs Cannon, Mojo, and Dr. Chubbs for enduring my time away from home while helping discover music, and, of course, the members of Linkin Park. We haven't spoken since the funeral, but I am honored to be part of the history of this incredible band. I hope my story of perseverance and finding one's way inspires someone to find their own.

Photo by Marselle Washington

ABOUT THE AUTHOR

JEFF BLUE is a multi-platinum A&R executive, producer, song-writer, music publisher, attorney, journalist, and manager whose acts have collectively sold over one-hundred million albums. He has been A&R at Warner Bros., RCA, Interscope, Atlantic, Virgin, Jive Records, and Zomba Music.

He received a BMI Song writer Award in 2008, a Hollywood Lifetime Achieve-ment Award in 2018, and a Music Influencer of the Year Award 2017. As a songwriter, he has been signed to Universal Music, Warner Chappell, Zomba, and BMG Music Publishing. His articles have been published in *Billboard* and *HITS*, and he has lec-tured internationally. In addition to Linkin Park, he's worked with Macy Gray, Limp Bizkit, Korn, Daniel Powter, the Last Goodnight, Hoobastank, Better Than Ezra, DJ Ashba, and co-music supervised Aaliyah's *Queen of the Damned* soundtrack. In 2020 he produced a music docuseries and finished his first screenplay. He lives in Los Angeles where he received his undergraduate degree at UCLA, and law degree from Loyola Law School.